Career Crafting the Decade After High School

PROFESSIONAL'S GUIDE

Cathy Campbell & Peggy Dutton

Copyright © 2015 by Cathy Campbell

Published by:
Canadian Education and Research Institute
for Counselling (CERIC)
18 Spadina Rd, Suite 200
Toronto, Ontario
M5R 2S7
Canada
website: www.ceric.ca
Email: admin@ceric.ca

Campbell, C. and Dutton, P.
Career Crafting the Decade After High School:
Professional's Guide

Layout Design: MeisterWorks Graphic Design
Photographs: Purchased from www.istockphotos.com

This material may be used, reproduced, stored, or transmitted for non-commercial purposes. However, the author's copyright is to be acknowledged. It is not to be used, reproduced, stored, or transmitted for commercial purposes without written permission from CERIC. Every reasonable effort has been made to identify the owners of copyright material reproduced in the publication and to comply with Canadian Copyright law. The publisher would welcome any information regarding errors or omissions.

All photos in this book are for illustrative purposes only. They are not actual photos of individuals mentioned.

ISBN 978-0-9811652-6-4

Contents

Preface v

Chapter One
Career Planning in the Contemporary Context

School to Work Transition Takes Longer 1
Identity Exploration 3
Fuzzy Career Plans 4
Labour Market Is Confounding 4
Career Journeys Are Unpredictable 6
The Career Myth Persists 7
Today's Career Journeys in a Nutshell 9

Chapter Two
Finding Their Place

The Process of Finding Their Place 12
Strategies for Finding Their Place 13
Navigating 13
Exploring 15
Drifting 17
Settling 20
Committing 23
Is One Strategy Better Than Another? 26

Chapter Three
The Impact of Internal Factors

Knowing What They Wanted 29
Tolerance for Ambiguity 37
Resistance Skills 40

Chapter Four
The Impact of External Factors

Messages 43
Financial Support 47
Emotional Support 48
Employment Opportunities 51

Chapter Five
Shifting Places

Drifting 57
Settling 58
Exploring 59
Do I Settle or Navigate? 59
Megan's Points of Transitions 60
Shifting Strategies and Influences 61

Chapter Six
Career Crafting Techniques

- Rethinking the Ways We Work with Young Adults 63
- Career Crafting Techniques 65
- Know That It Will Be a Journey 66
- Actively Look for What Sparks Your Interest 69
- Develop a "Shopping List" to Guide Your Journey 70
- Experiment with Intent 75
- Create Your Own "Lucky Breaks" 78
- Take Another Step 81
- Plan with a Pencil 82
- Do What You Love Somewhere in Your Life 84
- Parting Words 86

Notes 87

Resources

- Career Crafting Techniques 94
- The Career Myth 95
- Finding Satisfying Work: Which Strategies Are You Using? 96
- Shopping List 97
- Explore List 98

Preface

From the time they are born until the day they get their high school diploma, the educational path for many young people is straightforward and clearly defined. Career decisions are something for the distant future. Not so once they graduate. For many, post-secondary education is the expected next step. However, university or college doesn't necessarily answer the question about what direction they should follow. Many post-secondary graduates face a chasm between completing their education and finding a suitable place in the labour market.

I experienced this same gulf upon graduating with a BA in Canadian Studies. Like many young people today, getting a degree didn't help me translate my interests and skills into a satisfying career pathway. My own school-to-work transition was a long and painful one, a lengthy period of trial and error that eventually saw me complete a BEd specializing in outdoor and experience-based education and, a few years later, a master of social work. I eventually found satisfying work, first in adult education, and later as a career counsellor working with young adults and their parents.

As with many of my colleagues, I began my career counselling practice believing that it was my job to help young people find the career that would fit them best. By doing this, I hoped they could avoid the emotional turmoil that I had experienced as a young adult. It wasn't long, however, before I began to question how feasible it was to expect that 18- and 19-year-olds could choose long-term career paths that had any reasonable chance of being successfully carried through.

I had the good fortune to hear HB Gelatt and John Krumboltz speak at conferences where they introduced career counselling approaches that embraced uncertainty and unpredictability. Inspired by their novel approaches, I began what has turned into a decade-long pursuit to better understand how uncertainty and unpredictability can be wholistically incorporated into career counselling practice.

Gradually I evolved an approach—in the form of seven career design principles—that helped people proactively plan and do in the face of uncertainty and that emphasized the need to make informed choices while remaining open to change. I shared my model of practice in conference presentations and professional development workshops and was heartened to find that it resonated with many career practitioners.

Around the same time, I began to develop and pilot a program through the Nova Scotia Community College that articulated a constructive role that parents could play in their children's career development. A particularly striking revelation that surfaced from my discussions with parents was their expectation that their children's career would follow a linear, predictable route from high school to post-secondary education, and then on to a permanent, full-time job. They held this expectation despite the fact that they knew many people, sometimes including themselves, whose career pathways had been circuitous. I began referring to this unfounded supposition as the "Career Myth."

I became interested in furthering my understanding about the processes that young people engage in as they make and enact education and career-related decisions after finishing high school. In 2007, Dr. Michael Ungar and I were fortunate to receive funding from the Canadian Education and Research Institute of Counselling (CERIC) to undertake a qualitative study entitled *Stories of Transition* that involved 100 young people from four Canadian sites (Halifax, Guelph, Calgary, and rural Prince Edward Island).

Our research highlighted the reality that it is common for young people—even those who appear to be well-informed and focused—to spend many years after high school experimenting with post-secondary education programs and jobs, trying to figure out what constitutes satisfying work. We also found that young people used a variety of strategies to find their career-related place and that there were numerous internal and external factors and unpredictable events that impacted their career journeys.

Two publications were developed out of the findings that emerged from the research: *The Decade After High School: A Professional's Guide* and *The Decade After High School: A Parent's Guide*.

After the books were published, I was able to extend the findings of the *Stories of Transition* study as part of a PhD program at Massey University in New Zealand. An extensive review of the youth transition literature highlighted the contingent nature of many young adults' career journeys; revealed a host of internal and external factors and unexpected events that impacted the strategies that young people employed in their attempts to find a suitable career-related place, and backed the existence of the Career Myth. I undertook a more in-depth analysis of the study data in light of this scholarship which sharpened my understanding of the school-to-work transitions of the study participants.

My PhD work made it apparent that career professionals needed to have techniques to support young people in working with both the affective and cognitive aspects of unpredictability and non-linear change in relation to their career pathways. With this in mind, I refined the career design principles that had been developed earlier in my career and began offering them as an antidote to the Career Myth.

In 2014, CERIC invited me to update *The Decade After High School: A Professional's Guide* to ensure that the material continued to be relevant for career service providers working with teenagers and young adults. To this end, interviews and focus groups were conducted with young people and career professionals to check the findings of the original study and to get more insight into how service providers can help young people work with the uncertainty that is increasingly part and parcel of their career journeys.

The strategies and influences that were identified in the original study resonated with the young people that were interviewed this time around. They also confirmed the existence of the Career Myth and the anxiety it created for them after high school graduation.

The most challenging aspect of this project was the further reworking of the career design principles that ultimately became eight Career Crafting Techniques. My objective when developing the Techniques was that they remain true to my and other researchers' findings. I wanted to ensure that they placed uncertainty and unpredictability firmly in the forefront, and that they were practical to use, impactful, and spoke to young people's experiences. It is my sincere hope that career professionals will find the approaches presented in this book beneficial and that some of the strategies offered can be integrated seamlessly into their current practices.

As with any project of this magnitude, there are many people who have contributed to its creation. First, I would like to thank the young people from across Canada who participated in the original study and the subsequent follow-up. Their willingness to share their experiences and perspectives added a human dimension to the academic research and allowed me to shed more light on the complex and often turbulent time that occurs in the decade after high school. I'm also indebted to CERIC who made this project possible through their financial support.

I'm grateful to Dr. Ungar for his early input into the career design principles, for first suggesting that I undertake the *Stories of Transition* research project, and for being a co-author on the original *Decade After High School* publications.

A special thanks to Jeanette Hung who has played many roles in supporting my development as a career professional. It was through a chance encounter in an airport that I learned from her about a post-graduate career counselling internship opportunity at Dalhousie University. Jeanette's mentoring honed my counselling skills and provided a strong foundation in career development theory. She encouraged me to seek funding from CERIC for the *Stories of Transition* project and provided helpful feedback on the Career Crafting Techniques that are presented in this book.

Karen Schaffer, a gifted career counsellor at St. Mary's University, provided invaluable suggestions on how to make the Career Crafting Techniques more useful to counsellors and played a critical role in their refinement.

Lastly, my heartfelt thanks to Peggy Dutton. Our many conversations over the past 12 years have stretched my thinking about the realities of young people's career journeys and challenged me to develop an approach to practice that is practical without being simplistic. Her rich experience in career development and well-honed writing skills were in evidence as editor/co-author of the earlier *The Decade After High School* publications. This book would not have been possible without her.

Cathy Campbell, PhD
January 2015

Chapter One
Career Planning in the Contemporary Context

Eighteen and getting out of school, your whole world changes. It's a scary place.
∽ Raja, 24-year-old from Calgary

School to Work Transition Takes Longer

At one time, the majority of youth went straight from school to work with only a small minority attending post-secondary education. Due to the economic transformations of recent decades, higher levels of education and training have now become essential for opening up career options, sustaining employment, and improving earning powers.[1] Attending post-secondary has extended young people's transition to adulthood in a number of significant ways.

First, the programs themselves have become longer. On-the-job training and one-year certificates have become two-year diplomas. Rigorous certification processes have been tacked onto degrees for entrance into many regulated occupations. Undergraduate degrees have become the requisite norm to compete for spots in many professional programs.

This "credential inflation"[2] has turned a diploma or degree into the bottom line entry point for increasing numbers of jobs. But that's often not enough. When a bachelor's degree isn't sufficient, many young people feel compelled to pursue college technical training or continue onto advanced degrees at university, in an effort to improve their marketability or to progress to the top of their chosen professions.[3]

Then there are the young people themselves. Many young people enter post-secondary education with little or no idea of what they want to study. They use their time in college or university to test out different programs, discover their interests, see what might fit their abilities, and uncover education or career options they were unaware of.[4]

A fair amount of "milling and churning"[5] occurs as students drop out and re-enter at a later date, or as they switch programs and institutions in the hopes that their second/third choices are better matches. Exploration, re-evaluation, committing to a choice, and persisting to obtain a desired credential all add to a young person's transition timetable—and add to the cost. Many graduates (and those whose milling and churning hasn't resulted in a suitable educational choice) find themselves in serious debt.

Sometimes mounting debt makes it impossible for them to continue pursuing education which might improve their employment prospects.[6] They are forced to enter the workforce, take whatever employment they can, and begin the slow process of repaying student loans.[7] Others choose the opposite route: they stay in school for lack of a better option and to defer having to deal with job hunting and loan repayments.

Post-Secondary Education by the Numbers

82% high school graduates go to post-secondary within 3 years of graduating[8]

60% 25–34-year-olds have a college or university credential[9]

60% graduate from a different program than the one they entered[10]

25% try three or more programs[11]

70% first degree holders in the Maritimes return to get more schooling[12]

60% bachelor degree holders leave with student debt[13]

$28,000 average size of student debt in Ontario and the Maritimes[14]

10 years average time to pay off $28,000 @ $340/month[15]

18% people with university degrees who have jobs that require high school or less[16]

2 CAREER CRAFTING THE DECADE AFTER HIGH SCHOOL: PROFESSIONAL'S GUIDE

Milling and churning continues for many young people as they move from post-secondary education into the workforce. An Australian study found that, between the ages of 22 and 30, about 60% of the young people surveyed had held between two and four jobs and a further 20% had held five or more jobs.[17] Even some young adults who are working in what appear to be long-term jobs may, in fact, be milling and churning through the "guise of doing something likely considered to be more 'appropriate'."[18]

For some, "job surfing"[19] may relate to identity exploration as young people seek out different experiences as a way of helping them become clearer about who they are and what type of work they want to do. Even for those who follow a linear career pathway up to the point of graduation, a bleak job market may force them to move from one temporary job to another or take jobs outside their areas of study while continuing to seek full-time employment in their field.[20]

By the age of 30, many young people's careers have become more stable.[21] However, a substantial number continue to mill and churn, changing jobs because they haven't found anything that appeals, or because working conditions and/or pay are unacceptable.[22]

While milling and churning is common in western countries, it certainly isn't universal. Some young people continue to make remarkably linear school-to-work transitions.[23] This is particularly true for those who graduate with an occupationally-directed credential, such as engineering, licensed practical nursing, or carpentry, providing they can find employment in their field and enjoy the work once they are employed.

Identity Exploration

Jeffrey Arnett argues that the changes in the way young people transition into adult roles means that the period between the late teens and mid-twenties has become a distinct period developmentally.[24] Partially because suitable, sustaining employment depends on increasing amounts of education, young people are delaying getting married and having children. In 2008, the average age of first marriage in Canada was 31 for men and 29 for women, a significant increase from the early 1970s when first marriages occurred, on average, at 23 and 21 years respectively.[25]

In the past, the pressures of marriage and parenthood "forced" most young people to sort out how they were going to make a living in their late teens and early twenties. Without these responsibilities, young people have more time to explore who they are and what it is they want to do. Arnett has coined the term "emerging adulthood" to describe this period of exploration that many young people engage in between their late teens and mid-twenties.[26]

According to recent transition studies, the primary way that young people explore their identity is by trying things out.[27] They become clearer about their personal and work identities by engaging in different post-secondary education experiences, paid and unpaid work, and extracurricular activities. Just as importantly, they become more aware of what they don't want. As Arnett points out, explorations in emerging adulthood often include failure or disappointment which can be illuminating for self-understanding.

Some young people go about exploring in a systematic way, while others approach it more haphazardly.[28] Rather than carefully considering what might be promising options to explore, some young people opt for the post-secondary program or institution that is closest at hand, fall into jobs that happen to come their way, or are accidentally exposed to areas of interest through serendipitous experiences. While a haphazard approach may not be a particularly effective exploration strategy, it nevertheless does result in young people gathering more information about themselves and viable career options.

Identity exploration is not merely self-indulgence. The need to construct an identity is increasingly a requirement in a world that no longer offers young people a well-defined, clearly understood notion of who they are.[29] In the past, young people may have chafed or rebelled against the roles that were laid out for them. However, there were definite roles and prescribed pathways, limited though they may have been.

Today, when "anything goes," everything is possible. Faced with an open-ended array of options and decisions, many young people engage in journeys of personal and professional self-discovery in order to construct identities that have not been preordained.

On the other hand, not every young person has the liberty of engaging in identity exploration. Parenthood, social class, tolerance for instability, and cultural norms all impact the degree to which a young person can use their late teens and twenties as a period of exploration.[30] Some young people may be pressured by parents or other authority figures to pursue a particular career destination. Instead of developing their identity through a process of exploration, they adopt a "ready-made identity" that is "drawn from conformity to values and expectations of significant others."[31]

Fuzzy Career Plans

It may be supposed that a young person who is actively pursuing a career goal has engaged in some level of thoughtful career decision making. Separate studies conducted in Britain, Australia, and the United States question this assumption.[32] These studies found that most of their participants made decisions "based on weak commitments, fuzziness about the future, and limited information."[33]

The British study found that participants varied greatly in how they imagined their futures. While some had a relatively clear vision of a future that was probable, others had an image that was vague and full of uncertainties. Another group of participants had no imagined future at all that could be used to guide their decision making. The researchers concluded that the "unsearched, unstable or desperate choices" of participants were frequently turned into firm career decisions when factors, such as time constraints, unplanned events, and pressure from significant others, exerted their influence.[34]

Collectively, the findings of these studies question whether most young people choose a career direction in any meaningful way. Most select from the opportunities that are evident in their environment, rather than seeking out different ones that might be more satisfying. Choice, for many young people, is simply one in which they say "yes" or "no" to the opportunities that are readily available.[35]

The fact that many young people are following pathways without plans may be explained by making a differentiation between "career decidedness" and "career commitment."[36] Young people often find themselves in situations where circumstances force them to make a choice before they are ready to do so.

After graduating from high school, for example, they may feel compelled to choose a post-secondary program, even an occupationally-specific one like nursing, without having committed to a career in that field. According to this line of thinking, it is important not to confuse the commitment that a young person has to completing a particular program of studies with a committed choice to pursue an occupation associated with that training.

These research findings suggest that career decision making occurs in incremental stages, rather than through well-considered long-term planning. In fact, some studies found that, while participants were committed to their short-term plans, few had long-term visions about what they were hoping to do.[37]

This incremental style of decision making means that career selection is not a point in time event, but rather something that evolves. Instead of choosing a prescribed career pathway, many "produce" a unique career by engaging in an idiosyncratic combination of training, study, and employment.[38] This thinking aligns with career development theorists who have abandoned the construct of career because it connotes occupational and economic locations such as doctor, lawyer, engineer, or teacher that can't be achieved by most.[39]

Labour Market Is Confounding

For many, the labour market is a confusing and seemingly contradictory place. Changes in the Canadian economy have created new workforce dynamics that make it difficult to predict with any certainty what type of education and training will provide good employment. While many employers contend that they can't find people with the right qualifications, workers and would-be workers ponder why their degrees and diplomas aren't adequate.

The growth of a knowledge economy is creating what has been referred to as an "hourglass" labour market where jobs are grouped into three main categories: knowledge jobs, which require high skill levels and usually a post-secondary credential; middle-level jobs, which require work experience but not necessarily a degree or diploma; and entry-level jobs which usually require no previous work experience and a high school diploma or less.[40] The hourglass effect comes from being top and bottom heavy with stagnated growth in the middle.

While the number of knowledge sector jobs has increased substantially in the Canadian economy, so has the number of young people with university and college qualifications. As was said previously, credential inflation has become the standard hiring norm. Young people are faced with a situation where a college diploma or university degree is required to compete for many jobs, but there's no guarantee the credential will get them the job—or that they'll need their training to actually do the work, if hired.

Many of those post-secondary graduates who aren't able to gain access to the knowledge sector get stuck in entry-level jobs that require no more than a high school diploma. The highest incidence is amongst graduates of humanities, social science, and business administration programs.[41] Little wonder that many undergraduates, particularly those from liberal arts and science programs, return to school to get advanced degrees or technical diplomas in hopes of moving out of entry level jobs.[42]

What is perhaps most puzzling about the labour market is the assertion by many employers that they have a significant problem finding people with the right skills.[43] How can this be at the same time that so many young people with post-secondary qualifications say they can't find jobs that are commensurate with their training?

Rick Miner, a respected educator and management consultant, contends that there are several types of skills mismatches that lead to the phenomena of "people without jobs and jobs without people."[44] An obvious type of mismatch is geographical in nature, where the labour market supply and demand in a particular region doesn't align. Another type relates to young people having more qualifications than are required for the jobs they are hired to do.

A third type of mismatch that Miner describes is a supply/demand gap. Simply put, there are too many people trained for some types of jobs and not enough for others. Miner notes that labour market projections indicate there will be a higher demand for graduates with college, polytechnic, and trades credentials. Yet, university enrolments are increasing significantly more than their technical and applied arts/science institution counterparts.

He also points out that university enrolment in programs where there is higher labour market demand, such as science, technology, engineering, math, computer science, and information science, is far lower than in fields like humanities and social sciences. Graduates from general degree programs, and employers who could hire them, have more difficulty identifying what job-specific skills they possess and what employment opportunities might be an appropriate fit.[45] As a result these young people try, through a painful process of trial and error, to find a suitable place in the labour market.

Others argue that, when employers say they can't find qualified people, what they really mean is that they can't find people with prior experience doing the work they want done.[46] They claim that employers aren't looking to hire young workers right out of school. They want experienced candidates who can contribute immediately with no training or start-up time, which translates into people who have done virtually the same job before. The existence of an experience gap was borne out in an Ontario study which found that many employers advertising on three major Canadian career websites were demanding two, three, and even five years of work experience for their "entry level" jobs.[47]

Most young people have the same desire as previous generations to have "standard employment" characterized by full-year, full-time work with benefits and stability.[48] This goal, however, has been frustrated by economic and demographic realities.

A study in Southern Ontario found that half of the workers they surveyed were working full or part time with no

CHAPTER ONE 5

benefits or job security, or in temporary, contract, or casual positions.[49] Low-income workers in this group were typically employed by temporary agencies; in the fast food, cleaning, and service sectors, or in "on call" manufacturing jobs.

They also found that precarious employment was not the sole purview of low-income workers. Unstable funding and just-in-time hiring practices also impacted middle and even upper-income workers employed as university/college lecturers and research assistants, school teachers, hospital nurses, government personnel, and front-line professionals in non-profit agencies.

For the young person starting out, it can be a daunting task to assemble critical career launch qualifications out of low-skilled or precarious jobs that don't provide skills-enhancing training or experiences. Being underemployed on a long-term basis at the start of one's career can have enduring effects as young people struggle to ever catch up with older workers and their more "successful" peers. The debilitating consequences of prolonged underemployment can include: persistent earnings disparity, growing gaps in one's resume, deterioration of skills, erosion of confidence, anxiety, and uncertainty about the future.[50]

Career Journeys Are Unpredictable

If career choice and identity exploration are closely linked, it follows that a young person's choices will change as their identity evolves. Given that an individual's identity can change dramatically during the years of emerging adulthood, it isn't surprising that young people would find a career choice made at age 18 is no longer congruent with their identity a few years later.

With identity exploration, comes instability.[51] The only constant for many emerging adults is that their ideas keep changing. As they try things out, they learn more about themselves and the options available to them. New learning often leads them to change their plans.

They discover the computer science program they chose isn't as interesting as they had imagined and they're back scouring college calendars for a replacement. They learn their mediocre undergraduate grades won't get them into medical school and they have to abandon a career dream and seek another. They enter the workforce and are exposed to exciting opportunities that lead them off in completely new directions.

Identity exploration alone can't fully account for the large number of changes that many young people make in relation to their education and career journeys. In addition to interests, abilities, and values, a multitude of other factors influence the degree to which a young person is able to move along a chosen path. These can include factors related to family, peers, ethnicity, socioeconomic status, political decisions, and labour market conditions.[52]

Chance events also facilitate or constrain the career journeys young people undertake. These events can include: right time/right place scenarios; personal and professional connections; influences of marriage and parenthood, and career advancements, roadblocks, or exposure to new opportunities.[53] Unexpected events are so pervasive in the unfolding of a young person's career path that, according to John Krumboltz and Al Levin, they should be expected.[54]

With the existence of so many factors impacting on the progress of one's career journey it is little wonder that most young people's career decision making is fluid, unpredictable, and non-linear.

The Career Myth Persists

Compared to the supposed orderly, sequential pathways taken by previous generations, terms like floundering, lost, directionless, and on hold have been used to describe what the career journeys of today's young people look like.[55]

Many adults, with the sharp clarity of hindsight, would have to admit their own career journeys weren't all that orderly. Rather, they were filled with the twists and turns of misread directions, roadblocks, detours—and unexpected surprises along the way. Few are doing work today they could have predicted, or even imagined, they'd be doing when they were 20. For many, things didn't unfold as planned. Assuming there ever was a plan to begin with.

And yet, the "Career Myth" persists.[56] The Career Myth goes something like this: "Have a plan (preferably the right one and preferably made early), stick with it, and you'll proceed in a straight line from school to work to retirement."

Most parents, teachers, and counsellors are well aware that the landscape has changed dramatically in the past thirty years and would consider this an outlandish over-statement of their assumptions. Yet, there is still a widely-held expectation that young people will proceed, more or less, along this trajectory in what has been referred to as an "extended linear" model of transition.[57] This expectation is predicated on the assumption that there's a relatively simple relationship between qualifications and employment: getting a job follows from getting a qualification.

The Career Myth continues to pervade the narrative of parents' messages, advice, and reactions. It informs the way in which teachers and counsellors offer career advice to their students. It seeps into the very hearts and souls of young people, even though they (and most of their friends) haven't managed to stumble upon the magic formula to make it happen.

Annika, a 28-year-old who was working on her second master's degree after not finding satisfying work, spoke about the impact the Career Myth had on her:

It has affected me almost like an identity crisis. If you're not getting this good job, then what's going on? If you're not following this path, what's broken? What do you need to do to get back on track? Not getting that good job has pulled me back in being able to start a family and moving forward with my life.

Like many other myths, this one has some grounding in reality. Once upon a time, in the middle of the 20th century, many middle-class white men had career pathways that did lend substance to the myth's tenets. In a post-industrial age, the certainty that is embodied in the Career Myth no longer applies to most of those who are privileged, let alone those who aren't.[58]

But still, there are just enough "bright lights" around who appear to enact the Myth that people continue to believe it.[59] Because the Career Myth is considered the normal or correct way to make the school-to-work transition, it is held up by youth and those around them as the gold standard to which young people should aspire—and to which they are measured.[60]

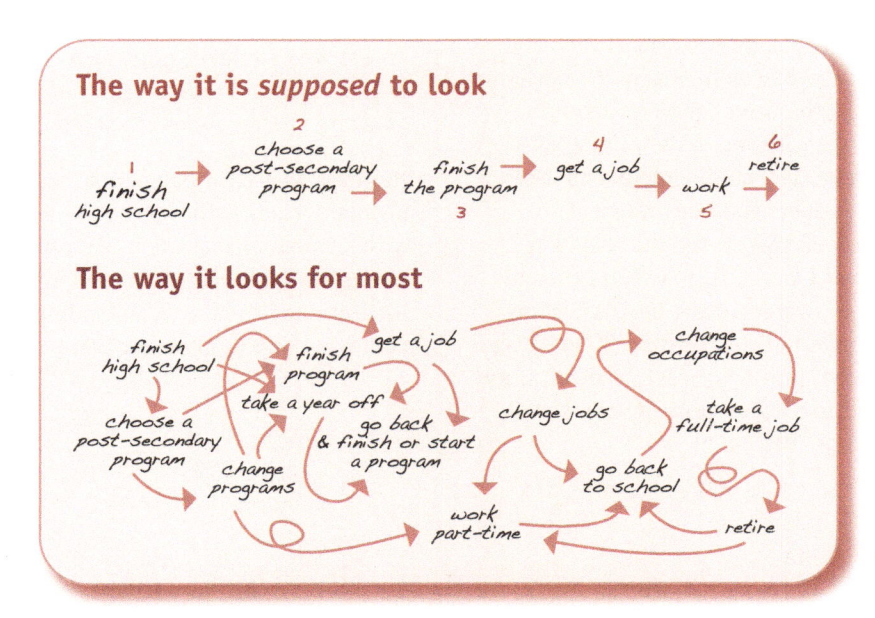

The way it is *supposed* to look

1. finish high school → 2. choose a post-secondary program → 3. finish the program → 4. get a job → 5. work → 6. retire

The way it looks for most

finish high school → choose a post-secondary program → change programs → finish program → take a year off → go back & finish or start a program → get a job → change jobs → go back to school → work part-time → change occupations → take a full-time job → retire

This material is available courtesy of the Government of Alberta, Ministry of Innovation and Advanced Education.

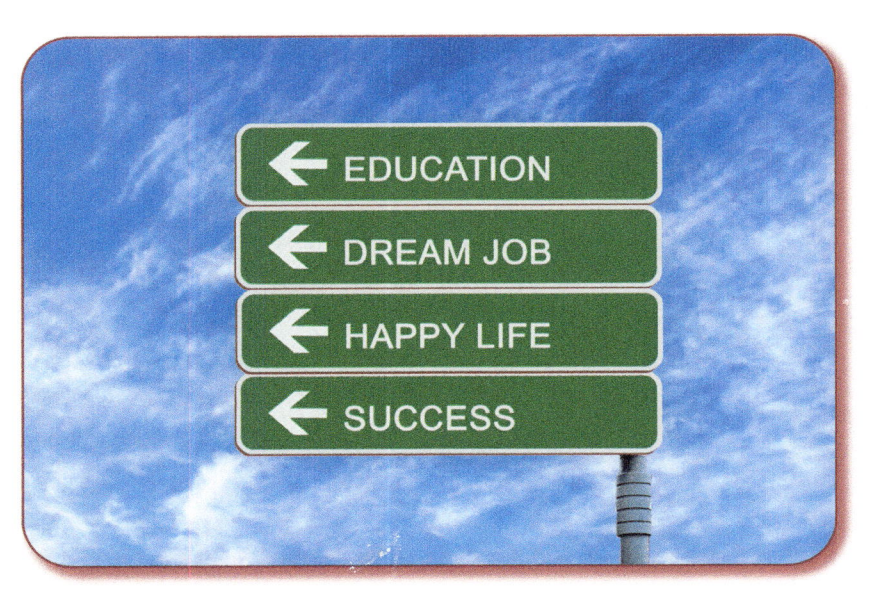

Unrealistic expectations about certainty

The Career Myth creates unrealistic expectations about the level of certainty young people should have about the nature of their own career journeys.[61] Given the powerful sway these expectations hold, it isn't surprising that young people often experience a great deal of pressure to have a career plan, despite the reality that many don't and most plans never unfold as envisioned.

More often than not, the expectation about having a plan isn't explicitly stated. But, when they are repeatedly asked, "What are you doing after graduation?" many young people interpret this as an expectation that they should have an answer.[62]

By having a plan, young people, parents, educators, and everyone else concerned can be comforted by the illusion the Career Myth offers up. The Career Myth encourages what has been referred to as "closed-system thinking"[63] whereby individuals believe they have complete control over what happens. They expect their environment to function in a stable and predictable way and they don't acknowledge the myriad of factors, such as bad luck and fickle labour markets, that can derail the best laid plans. Closed-system thinking about career decisions "run(s) the risk of lulling the individual into a false sense of certainty, or limiting the individual to an unnecessarily constrained and unimaginative range of choices."[64]

When young people compare their career progression to normative assumptions, most will perceive theirs to be disordered.[65] Little wonder then that many young people feel anxious. Anxious if they don't have a plan; anxious wondering if the plan is the right one; anxious when the plan doesn't work out, and anxious if they change their plan and face the disappointment or disapproval of those closest to them. Perhaps most perturbing, they blame themselves: "I thought doing everything I was told would lead to a successful, satisfying life but it isn't working. It must be my fault."

Krumboltz maintains that procrastination is one way that young people attempt to manage the anxiety they feel about their career journeys.[66] Because the Career Myth leads young people to believe that their career decisions must be right from the outset, some are afraid to make a decision for fear it is the wrong one. Others manage their discomfort by readily choosing a career direction without spending the time to investigate whether their choice is a good fit. They are so relieved after making a decision that many "push it to the far recesses of the mind so they don't have to be anxious about it anymore."[67]

For many, having an ironclad plan is the antidote for dealing with the unrealistic expectations of the Career Myth. The education system teaches young people to plan. The ones who plan most effectively are "successful." As Jenn Davies, a manager of career development services at the University of Toronto has observed, they move from the grade school plan to the post-secondary school plan and "those who are really good at following the get-good-grades-in-sequenced-courses plan go on to professional or graduate studies, where they follow more plans."[68]

However, as Davies points out, at some point most young people, including those who are expert planners, are faced with the reality that there is no pre-packaged "rest of your career life" plan. For those still attached to an educational institution, this may mean landing at the counsellor's door—looking to make another plan.

Today's Career Journeys in a Nutshell

Taking all the recent research into consideration, what do the career journeys of many young people look like? Lengthy stints in training institutions. Student debt that takes years to pay off. Endless sifting and sorting through an overwhelming number of options to find a fit. Putting marriage and family on hold. Pressure to settle on a plan. Anxiety about making "right" decisions. An enigmatic labour market.

This portrait stands in sharp contrast to the image that many older adults hold of young people being unmotivated, entitled, and unwilling to grow up. There may be some justification in thinking that young people have had things pretty cushy. Maybe they have. Up until now. But, as emerging adults, they are confronted with challenges that previous generations didn't have to face.

It can be a scary, angst-ridden time when school ends, life is supposed to begin, and reality sets in. J.N. Salter, a 25-year-old blogger for the Huffington Post, described her reality shock after graduating from university:

Disney movies, our parents' expectations, and childhood platitudes ("Just think positive, things will work out, something will turn up, look on the bright side") don't prepare most of us for our 20s. No one warns us that "dream jobs" are a myth. We do not learn about unemployment and debt, loneliness, and structural inequality. Instead, we are told to get good grades so that we can go to a good college and get a good job and find a good husband or wife. Where is the Dr. Seuss book on what to do when your reality seems to consist of a bunch of unmet expectations—unemployment, a job you tolerate, debt you can't afford to pay, a relationship status that makes you want to deactivate your Facebook?[69]

Chapter Two

Finding Their Place

*What am I doing with my life? What do I want to do with my life?
Those are important questions, but they do take time to figure out.*
~ Bonita, 25-year-old from Guelph

As shown in Chapter One, the late teens and twenties can be a chaotic time. This was certainly the case for many of the participants in this study. The majority of young people interviewed either didn't have plans when they graduated from high school, or they changed their plans as experience caused their goals to shift or their access to resources such as education, employment opportunities, and emotional support grew or diminished.

Although their life stories were very different, the participants shared at least one common struggle after high school graduation: they wanted to "find a place" and, for them, place meant a career. While the term "career" is understood in the career development field as an individual's life-long progression in learning and paid employment, most participants defined career in terms of an end point, rather than a process. None of the participants considered their education to be part of their career and they sharply delineated the differences between having a career and a job.

The three most commonly cited criteria for having a career related to it being long term, providing financial stability, and being something the participants were passionate about doing. An additional criterion cited by a few participants was that a career was work that would gain them respect from other people.

Jordan, an assistant manager with a telecommunications company, considered his work was a "very well-paying job." In making the distinction between his job and a career, he incorporated all four criteria:

Something that I can comfortably live with financially and personally, as well as being able to deal with for another fifty years or forty years. Something that earns you respect, that somebody would look at you and say, "He's got a career."

For a few participants like Anthony, a dental technologist, financial security was the only measuring stick when gauging a career:

A career is something there's always going to be a need for. A job, you can get terminated, fired. I've had jobs. I worked at Canadian Tire: any monkey who is trained could do it. I worked at a call centre. That was a little more towards a career but, again, there was always a constant fear: if I don't do this perfect or somebody comes along that's better than me, I'm going to get canned. Where I'm at now, I don't have that worry. I can always go ahead and better myself.

Two young women travelling very different courses—Claire, a fitness trainer without job security and Stacey, a stay-at-home mom—both considered their jobs to be careers, on the sole basis that they were passionate about what they were doing.

The idiosyncratic ways in which participants defined career meant that only they could determine whether or not they had found a career-related place. Rebecca noted that others might assume that her job as a support worker for autistic children was a career because many of her colleagues viewed it that way:

My co-workers are where they want to be and this is going to be their career for the next twenty or thirty years. For me, it's a job because I know it's only going to be another year before I do some more school to move toward something else.

Finding a career-related place was seldom straightforward as participants tried to find a fit between what they wanted and the resources they had available. The good news was that, by the time these young adults were in their late twenties, the majority had found a place with which they were satisfied. A few found that place in their early twenties, but most needed more time. There was still, however, a sizeable minority who, for various reasons, weren't able to follow the route they had chosen or were still unclear about what they wanted to do.

The Process of Finding Their Place

While the study sought to understand how young people made career decisions, the data analysis indicated that career choice was a way participants confirmed and expressed their evolving identity. During the decade after graduation, they had much to learn about themselves and the opportunities that were available to them. As Vito expressed it:

While I was in school, I didn't know what I really wanted to do. I needed to get outside the four walls of high school to find out how things really work, to find out if I wanted to buy a house, live in an apartment, have the same job, a bunch of jobs. Having some deciding time helps you figure these things out.

For most, finding a place was the result of engaging in a process of trial and error. As they tried out different post-secondary education programs and types of work, they began to get a better sense of who they were and where they wanted to go career-wise. Some participants recounted stories of feeling they had found their place when something in their lives "felt right."

Colin's experience was illustrative. He had worked at different hotel jobs and even owned a shop in a hotel. When he returned to working as a waiter, he realized:

It's not what I'm doing; it's being in the hotel. It clicked for me instantly. I love it because it's like a village. You've got the housekeepers, maintenance people, kitchen, front desk, sales, and HR. You've got tons of different people, different parties, conventions. You have things that have to be fixed all the time. I love the energy.

For others, where they wanted to be changed over time as their identity evolved. This was the case for Torin who, at 27, said: "I think I've only really become comfortable with who I am and who I see myself being in terms of my career, probably in the last year."

Strategies for Finding Their Place

A key finding of the study was that participants rose to the challenge of finding a career-related place—more or less successfully—by using five different strategies:[1] navigating, exploring, drifting, settling, and committing. The first three, navigating, exploring, and drifting, relate to the way that participants searched for their place. The last two, settling and committing, refer to how they engaged with the place they had found.

It was not uncommon for participants to use different strategies either simultaneously or successively. For example, some were simultaneously navigating and exploring. They had stated a career goal and had started to navigate towards it by enrolling in the required training, at the same time they were using the education experience to explore whether or not their choice fit with their evolving identity.

Others successively used (and re-used) different strategies as circumstances unfolded. They may, for example, have started to navigate toward a post-secondary program; been declined admission; navigated successfully through another program; taken a job in their field of study and been laid off; settled for an unsatisfying job as a survival necessity, and begun exploring for better options.

Hence, the typology is offered as a reference map to understand how young people go about finding a place, rather than an attempt to definitively categorize the activities of particular young adults.

Navigating

When participants used a navigating strategy, they knew what they wanted to do and were undertaking education, work, or other activities necessary to progress on their journey. Sometimes they had some prior exposure to their educational or occupational choice, or they had some assistance in identifying options that fit their interests and abilities. In many cases, they didn't.

Most didn't know much about the specifics of what they had chosen to do. That left a strong element of chance to determine whether their navigating would succeed. Would they get into the training program they wanted? Would they like the program and be successful? Would they find a job in the field they had chosen? Would they enjoy the work?

Consequences of navigating

The consequences of navigating varied dramatically among participants. For Kristen and those like her, navigating was a highly efficient method of directly transitioning from education programs that they liked and excelled at into work that was interesting and satisfying. Others who used a navigating strategy ended up switching programs or working in their chosen field of study and regretting every minute of it.

Participants who used a navigating strategy straight out of high school were inclined to end up somewhere they didn't want to be. More often than not, participants told stories of having chosen a field only to discover that the realities of the work weren't what they had imagined. Phillip, who was working as a landscaper, described navigating towards computer networking only to find out that it wasn't something he enjoyed:

When I went to university, computers were the thing, so that's what I did. Thinking, I like to play computer games, I'll love computer science. Not the same thing at all. I went to university for three years and I got my certificate in computer science, which is now just a real expensive banner on the wall.

After that, I went to work for a professor, installing coding software. That's when I decided I hate computers. Not really hate them, but I just couldn't…

I grew up doing forestry for my father. I'm used to working outside with my hands, doing a lot of physical labour stuff. So I was inside doing the computer and I looked at all the kids walking around campus on a nice day. It was just hard on my head.

It really wasn't me. I could do it, but I really didn't like it. I made great money, but I just couldn't stand it. I'd rather make way less money for something that I like to do.

Like many high school graduates, Phillip chose to pursue an occupation that he knew little about. As he found out, this can lead to expensive learning. Val learned the same hard lesson. She navigated directly toward office administration after high school. By the time she realized she didn't like working in an office, she had amassed a $20,000 student debt. Ten years later, she still owed $18,000—for a diploma she never used.

For some, particularly those who had navigated to what might be considered "good" occupational goals such as nursing, computer science, or engineering, the realization that they had chosen the wrong destination could become "a trap." How could they not follow through? How could they turn their backs on the potential earnings or face the disappointment of others?

Those who had been single-minded in their goals were often left anxious and confused when their navigating plans were side-swiped. Vanessa's high school dream had been to become a doctor. When she wasn't accepted into medical school, she became "bogged in the mud" and she spent years drifting and exploring before she discovered another option that she wanted to pursue.

Case Study – Navigating

Kristen was a 24-year-old working in Calgary as a chemical engineer with a large petrochemical company. She enrolled in a university chemical engineering program immediately after high school and found a job in her field soon after graduation.

At the beginning of Grade 12, I had no clue what I wanted to go into, but I was leaning towards chemistry. [In] meetings with my guidance counsellor, I was discussing that I was thinking chemistry and he suggested getting into engineering. When the university was doing their open house for high school students, I went to both presentations and, from that, decided whole-heartedly that engineering was the way to go.

While Kristen appeared to know exactly what she wanted to do coming out of high school, she said that she hadn't been certain about her decision. She had to experience the engineering field through her university courses and co-op placements to confirm that being an engineer was a good career choice for her.

Even though I didn't know what I wanted to do for sure, I thought it was a good opportunity. I don't even know if I knew back then that engineers can do so many different jobs.

Kristen was enjoying her job at the time, but she fully expected to be doing other types of work within the engineering field in the future.

Analysis: Kristen took an unusually direct route from high school to university and into a full-time job that she found satisfying. This was possible because she had all the necessary resources to start her journey and follow through to her goal:

- She had the *self-awareness* in high school to know that her interests and abilities lay in math and chemistry.
- With the *help* of a guidance counsellor, she was able to translate those interests and abilities into a post-secondary program that was a good fit.
- Kristen's parents *supported* her decision to choose engineering and *paid* the costs associated with her getting a degree. This meant she didn't need to work while attending university and could focus on her studies.
- Throughout university, Kristen was able to continually reconfirm her interests through her *experiments* with coursework and co-op practicums.
- Her *academic skills* and *motivation* helped her to successfully meet the rigorous requirements of completing an engineering degree.
- Because of the high *labour market* demand for engineers in Alberta, Kristen easily found satisfying employment directly related to her training after she graduated.

If any of these resources had not been available, Kristen's journey might not have been so straightforward. Without the assistance of a guidance counsellor, she would likely not have known in Grade 12 that engineering was a good fit with her interests and abilities. If she had followed her original plan to study chemistry, she still might have come to realize that engineering was a good fit, or she may have found an equally satisfying career in the field of chemistry. It would, however, almost certainly have taken her more exploration time or more years of training to do so.

Her parents' support was critical. Kristen said that she wouldn't have pursued engineering if they hadn't approved. Likewise, without a demand for chemical engineers, she would have been forced to either relocate or go into a different career field.

Kristen also enjoyed an element of *luck*. By her own admission, she knew little of what engineers did when she chose the occupation. She could have just as easily discovered that it wasn't something that interested her, or that another career field interested her even more.

Exploring

Exploring, as a strategy, occurred when participants couldn't say specifically what they wanted to do, but they were actively engaged in a process of research and experimentation as a means to learn more about themselves and their career options. They were proactive in their search for information about career opportunities; they speculated about areas of interest, and they sought experiences whereby they could conduct trial runs to determine the fit of particular options to their interests and abilities.

Exploring is critical for young people to determine, with any level of confidence, that the choices they make have a reasonable chance of being satisfying ones. It does, however, take time to know yourself and investigate career options well enough to make informed decisions. On the other hand, time can start slipping away. Some participants who had moved into their mid-to-late twenties were starting to feel that the opportunity for exploration was shrinking and it was time to start navigating.

Consequences of exploring

The consequences of exploring were generally positive for those participants who employed the strategy. One of its main benefits was the opportunity to feel out an option before making a commitment, at the same time staying open to new possibilities. Through the process of exploring, participants often realized it wasn't what they expected. It was generally easier for them to change their minds when they didn't feel bound to a choice. Rebecca described how her friend narrowly missed making a costly mistake:

She decided that she wanted to become a teacher. It was too late to apply to teaching school, so she looked for jobs teaching and got a job at a private school. She hated it. If she had gotten into teacher's college, she would have spent the year there and then found that she hated it. So, sometimes it's nice to dabble a little before committing yourself to a degree or certificate.

With increased self and career awareness gained through exploration, many participants felt more confident in the decisions they ultimately made. Vanessa described why she needed to go through the exploration process before enrolling in a public relations program:

I'm a very methodical person so I needed to think things through before I said, "Okay, I'm going back to school." I needed to know that I was really making the right decision. I've done a lot of things on a whim and I just didn't want this to be one of them. Now I'm more certain of who I am as a person, so I wanted to make sure this decision reflected that.

On the downside, participants who used an exploration strategy were often subjected to criticism, particularly if the exploring occurred outside of a post-secondary institution. Carol experienced parental criticism when she left college to work in retail. Her father told her, "I didn't move to Canada from Italy to not give you guys the better opportunity, so take advantage of it."

Case Study—Exploring

Carol, a 24-year-old from Calgary, had been working as an administrative assistant for two years with an oil company. She loved her work and the interaction she had with people. Carol wasn't sure what she wanted to do after graduating from high school, but she was interested in exploring the possibilities:

I did a bit of research, but I just wanted to see what would interest me. I thought, "I speak Italian fluently, so Spanish might be fun to learn." I was considering sports medicine all through high school. I played sports since I was 14 and I still kick box. So I started taking the sciences and that didn't appeal to me.

I couldn't find anything that I really was interested in at the college. I started looking at programs that another college does. I started doing more and more research.

I thought about being a pastry chef because I have a sweet tooth. Then I thought about being a chef and maybe owning my own restaurant. I do love to cook. That still intrigues me. But, the more I researched, I realized getting up at three in the morning to own your own bakery, not if I want kids. I like my Monday to Friday, nine to five.

Still unsure after a year at college, Carol decided to take some time off to figure out what she wanted to do. She took a job in retail and, in the process, learned a lot about herself:

I realized that I do like to work with people. I am very much a customer person. I have a bubbly, outgoing personality so I realized that I didn't want to be stuck by myself at a job. That eliminated a lot of different careers where you're on your own.

My brother's an accountant: I find it's pretty mundane. I like administration because it's very fast-paced and you're constantly multi-tasking...very interactive with other people.

Carol's retail job made her realize that she wanted regular working hours and a higher salary. Her brother, who worked in the oil and gas sector, encouraged her to consider that industry as a possibility. With that in mind, Carol decided to go back to school.

A college admissions officer suggested she take an information management program that would provide a "good starting place" and improve her computer skills. Carol was attracted to the program because it offered hands-on learning, the possibility of working in jobs where there was a lot of people contact and, as a final bonus, elective courses in office applications in the oil and gas industry.

Despite all the pluses going for the program, Carol still wasn't positive that office administration was the right choice for her. She viewed the program as an opportunity to test the depth of her interest in this career field. It was only through her practicum experience that she was able to confirm that office administration was the route she wanted to go.

Analysis: Like most young people who employ the exploring strategy, Carol was curious about where her interests and talents could best be put to work. She wasn't in a rush to make a decision and was willing to entertain and evaluate the possibility of a number of options. Carol employed the following exploration methods to increase self and career awareness:

- Using her *known* interests and abilities as a reference point, Carol developed a list of career possibilities.
- Through an initial negative college *experience*, she learned where her interests did not lay.
- She *investigated* another education institution, *researched* a number of programs, *generated* further possibilities, and *evaluated* them against her interests and the lifestyle she envisioned for herself.
- She took a work *time-out* which helped her confirm that she wanted her career choice to be compatible with her personality traits.
- Her brother assisted her in several ways. *Exposure* to his career choice confirmed what she didn't want. His industry *knowledge* opened her eyes to a new option.
- College personnel provided *guidance* which helped her identify a program that was potentially a suitable match.
- She enrolled in the college program, not as a set-in-concrete decision, but as another means to *explore* for fit. It was the practicum component of the program that clinched the deal for her.

Carol's exploration was also facilitated by her personal attributes:

- She was able to *resist* her parents' pressure to complete her original college program choice when she knew it wasn't right for her.
- She was willing to tolerate some *uncertainty* when she enrolled in the office administration program, considering she wasn't absolutely sure it was what she wanted.
- Even when office administration seemed compatible, given her interests and abilities, Carol didn't make a committed decision: she remained *open to change* if she found something that interested her more.

Drifting

Participants who used a drifting strategy didn't know what they wanted to do, were laissez-faire about making choices, or faced numerous barriers to implementing their plans. Being unable or unwilling to proactively seek a career direction, they were apt to "go with the flow." Over time, some became stuck. There was a sense of aimlessness and passivity in the stories that participants who were drifting told of their post-secondary education and work histories.

The typical image of a young person adrift is someone who is wasting their time engaged in menial jobs, or not working at all. However, drifting isn't always that easy to spot. From the outside, most people around Antoine would have assumed that he was an ambitious young man getting a university degree and going to work in his father's successful business. He appeared to be on track towards a satisfying career while, in fact, he was without direction. Antoine was engaged in what we refer to as "high-functioning drifting."

Graduate and professional schools are favorite hang-outs for high-functioning drifting. It's tempting for university students with good grades to defer the uncertainty of making career decisions by simply continuing to go to school. It was like that for Chris who received funding to pursue a master's degree that covered his tuition and living expenses. He explained what motivated him to enrol in graduate studies:

When I did my undergrad, I did a few co-op work terms and they provided very low job satisfaction. I don't even know why I did computer science. I never owned a computer in my life.

I always did well in school, so one of the professors said I should apply for a scholarship for graduate school. I got a full scholarship, so school was for free anyway. I ski a lot and there's better skiing in Calgary. I could go anywhere, so I decided to go to university in Calgary.

Consequences of drifting

It's natural to assume that drifting is not a good thing. Certainly drifting for long periods of time isn't likely to lead to satisfying work. However, drifting can have its place as a legitimate career search strategy. For some participants, drifting unaware into a post-secondary education program, "falling into" a job, or taking a time-out proved to be a form of passive exploration where they were exposed, purely by chance, to new experiences. Rebecca described how drifting helped her learn more about herself:

I feel more secure in my values and what I want to have in my life. Even after university, I didn't feel I really knew myself. It took travelling and time off and different jobs to help me figure that out. I just needed more life experience between university and now.

Several participants accidentally bumped into previously-unknown career options that proved to be just what they were seeking. Ironically, had they been using a navigating or exploring strategy, they would likely have missed out on these opportunities.

This was the case for Anthony, a dental technologist. After high school, Anthony opted to work at jobs that were "at hand" with the vague notion of saving money, but with no career goal in mind. Purely by accident, he came across an offer of training in a career field he knew nothing about and had no reason to think would be interesting:

Going through a web site I found this listing for a dental lab and they said on-the-job training provided. It's like, "Okay, why not? That's a job where they don't want somebody to Mickey Mouse around." That's why I took the job. And they've lived up to it. It was the biggest fluke of my life.

While drifting opens the door to serendipitous encounters, it does pose dangers if it goes on for an extended period of time. A few participants in their late twenties had obtained little in the way of qualifications or marketable skills a decade after they had graduated from high school.

Case Study—Drifting

Antoine was a 27-year-old from Guelph who had been working for his father in the real estate and construction field for the past three years. He didn't particularly enjoy the work he was doing, but he wasn't sure what else to do. Antoine explained how he drifted into university and then into his present job:

When I was going into university, I didn't have something in mind that I wanted to be. From high school, I had good grades and obviously it was the logical decision. If you have the means, go to university and take the next step.

I ended up being at university for five years. Whatever it was—lack of motivation, ambition, direction, goal setting—I still graduated not knowing what I wanted to do. I had a diploma, but I didn't know what I wanted to do with it. Applying for jobs afterwards was, as you would imagine, difficult because there wasn't a clear direction that I wanted to go.

I tried applying to law school. Law school was not necessarily something that I wanted to do myself, but something that my father had pushed for. I'm sure there are many psychological reasons—to appease another individual, or trying to make them proud of you, or whatnot. Regardless, I didn't end up getting into law school.

I tried applying to a handful of jobs through web sites, which wasn't successful at all. I figured with my degree in English and political science that would be enough to apply to something within the government sector. I felt it would have been a job that would have been rewarding and fulfilling. Being a government job, it would pay relatively well.

I was sort of naïve. It's incredibly difficult to get into government if you don't have any connections. What I went through was discouraging and I don't think I exercised all the avenues open to me in order to perform a successful, not just job search, but career search.

I ended up getting discouraged and took a job working at the mall selling shoes. Not my proudest moment but, at the same time, I needed money and I found myself stuck in a rut. I quit after eleven months and decided I would either continue my career search or try something different.

My dad was a real estate agent and I ended up getting into business with him. Feel it was like a consolation that's available: it's easy to do so let's go for it.

After two years, it was a bit of a dead end. It wasn't something that I was passionate about; it wasn't something that was fulfilling. When my father suggested that I do real estate, it wasn't something that I necessarily wanted to do, but I felt that I couldn't say "no."

Analysis: As the eldest male from a Middle Eastern family, Antoine was expected to listen to his parents in his choice of a professional career, such as law, or by going into the family business.

- Antoine hadn't developed a strong sense of identity and *didn't know what he wanted* to do.
- He *drifted* into university and graduated no wiser about a career direction.
- He applied to law school for which he had *no particular interest*.
- Antoine had a rather *simplistic understanding* of the labour market and didn't realize that, with a general

CHAPTER TWO 19

university degree, he and prospective employers would have a difficult time relating his qualifications to suitable job prospects.

- By his own admission, Antoine was *passive* when it came to exploring a wider range of employment possibilities where his qualifications might have applied and he might have found satisfying work.
- He *settled* instead for an unfulfilling, but convenient job in retail.
- He accepted his father's job offer as a *ready-furnished* solution to his unsatisfactory work situation.
- Antoine was caught in a Catch-22 situation: without a sense of what he wanted, he found it difficult to *resist* his father's *expectations*. His father's expectations, on the other hand, made it difficult for Antoine to engage in an exploration process to figure out what he did want. So he remained *stuck* in a career field that held no appeal for him.

Settling

Participants who used a settling strategy had found a career-related place that they didn't particularly like but, for various reasons, they planned to stay. A decade after graduating, some participants had settled, attaching themselves to occupations or lifestyles that fulfilled their need for a place, but which they described as only being moderately satisfying. Their dissatisfaction may have come from the work itself, poor pay, or lack of potential for advancement.

Settling is common when a young adult has family responsibilities and bills to pay, but isn't able to find work that relates to their training or interests. Another reason for settling is that people have different motivations and place different value on working. It isn't everybody's priority to have a job that one's passionate about. Scott, a naval electronics engineering technician, explained that financial stability and the lifestyle that afforded him were his primary considerations:

I don't dislike my work, but I wouldn't say I enjoy it. It's something I do. I guess there are people who take a lot of enjoyment out of what they do for a living. For me, this is a means to live my life the way I want. It allows me to be comfortable financially, to pursue my hobbies, diving, volleyball, things I want to do outside of work.

The thought of leaving a job, even one that's unfulfilling, can be scary and overwhelming. For some participants, fear of the unknown prompted them to settle for the jobs they had. Anthony clung to long-held career dreams, but he spoke about why he chose not to take action:

I know what I'd like to do and I know what I'm doing. I cherish the idea of being an oceanographer, a geologist, or that type of thing. For now, it's just going to be off to the side. If I see a road that goes down that way, I might be tempted. But then again, I'm mostly driven by my fears. What happens if I lose my career? What happens if I take this leap of faith and I end up falling a couple hundred feet on my nose?

Consequences of settling

Participants reacted in different ways to settling. For some, it was quite demoralizing to have spent all that time and money only to discover they couldn't find work that used their credentials, or the career they had chosen wasn't satisfying. Taylor described what it was like having to settle for a "nothing" job:

When you're in university, you have this sense of purpose all the time. You're working towards this goal. When I got out of university and my dream job fell through, I was just working in a menial job that meant absolutely nothing to me and going nowhere. That was difficult and it still is. To work with no actual purpose other than to pay my rent and keep me clothed and fed. That's difficult.

Participants who had settled for jobs that provided security and good pay were often satisfied with the trade-off, particularly if they had family responsibilities. Maggie, who had recently married, said she was reasonably content with leaving a fast-paced, satisfying job for a more secure, but less challenging one:

I wanted to be able to spend time with my husband and he's new to the country. I just thought, "If I'm always stressed about work and coming home late every night, that's no fun." If I was single, I think this job would bore me out of my mind. But now, I have a lot of other things in my life. In terms of days off, overtime, vacation, I can't ask for anything more. But I hoped there would be room to advance or take on more things.

CHAPTER TWO 21

Case Study—Settling

Gabriela was 24 years old and working as a labourer in a furniture factory in Guelph. After high school, she obtained a college diploma in business administration, but was only able to find a job as a retail clerk. Her chance for advancement fell through when the store underwent a management change.

I was working at a department store and they asked me if I wanted the opportunity to work as a supervisor or assistant supervisor. A couple of weeks after they asked me, new management came in and stopped all the training. They wanted to focus on getting the store up to where it was supposed to be.

Disappointed and frustrated by losing the chance to move ahead, Gabriela quit her job. She recounted the difficulty she had finding work in her field:

I don't know if it's just this area, but finding a good job is hard. You can hand your resume out to every company in town and they're all like, "Oh sorry, you don't have enough experience." Well, I have all the requirements your job has asked for, how is it that I don't have enough experience?

Gabriela went on to describe how she ended up working in the factory and how she felt about the job:

I got into it by somebody who I used to work with. The job I was at, they weren't paying enough and my boyfriend and I had just gotten the house. It was like everything all at once: they paid a lot more and it was closer to where we were moving. So it was just convenience. At the time it was like, "How am I supposed to say no?"

I feel like I'm so much, it's bad to say, smarter than everybody else. I can count on one hand how many people who have some college, high school, or anything like that.

While Gabriela felt let down and underemployed working at the factory, she planned to stay because she had other responsibilities:

This job, yeah. It's not just me I'm thinking about now. I have to think about my boyfriend and we want to start a family. So it's not just me: it's somebody else too. But we've both made sacrifices.

Analysis: Gabriela's reason for settling for a job she didn't like is a common one. As young people move into their mid-to-late twenties, they are more likely to be in significant relationships. The focus begins to shift from "me" to "us." Gabriela's priorities had turned to paying the mortgage and eventually starting a family. Finding a job she liked had become of secondary importance.

- Gabriela's slide into settling mode was initiated by a promotion *opportunity falling through* and the tight *labour market* conditions in her area, two conditions over which she had no control.
- She had become *discouraged* trying to find suitable work and had *refocused* her interests on other aspects of her life.
- Gabriela hadn't completely given up on the idea of finding more satisfying work. She had *settled for now*, but was hopeful that, over time, an administrative position would open up at the factory. As well, she was planning to take bookkeeping courses in the future in an effort to improve her chances of securing more rewarding employment.

Committing

Participants who used a committing strategy had arrived at a career-related place that connected with them, one they were generally happy with, and had no plans to change any time soon. The good news was that, a decade after graduating from high school, many of the participants in this study had achieved a meaningful sense of place to which they were committed.

Those participants who had attained satisfying work had found something that fit their developing identity. However, over time, their chosen field or particular job might fit less well. Part of the reason this happens is that identity development doesn't stop in our late twenties. While it is most dramatic in our late teens and twenties, our identity continues to evolve. New interests and competencies may develop that lead us to explore and/or navigate towards other options in a related field or in a completely different direction.

Alternatively, things we used to enjoy may simply become stale over time. Anwar, an engineer, said:

Now that I've been in the same job for three, four years, I'm not sure if there's any more room for growth. Maybe I need to do a lateral shift to something in a different field or something just different. I've learned everything I can for this job, so do I move somewhere else in the company or do I move to a different company? I've hit that wall just recently, actually.

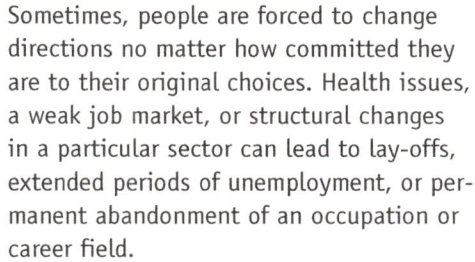

Sometimes, people are forced to change directions no matter how committed they are to their original choices. Health issues, a weak job market, or structural changes in a particular sector can lead to lay-offs, extended periods of unemployment, or permanent abandonment of an occupation or career field.

Consequences of committing

The main consequence for participants who used a committing strategy was that they had arrived at a place that they enjoyed and found fulfilling. This could be seen in Shawn, the chartered accountant, when he described how much he liked the variety of his work responsibilities.

Not surprisingly, participants who found their work meaningful were proactive about developing their proficiencies and building their careers. Anthony described his attitude shift once he discovered work for which he had enthusiasm:

I definitely put in a lot more overtime now because I'm driven. If I have a problem that needs to be fixed or something that needs to go out to a patient, I will work six, seven hours of overtime. I've had weeks when I've had 16 hours of overtime.

Working at the hardware store, if somebody said, "Hey, you want to work overtime?" I would probably say "no." I figured I put enough of my time into that. With what I do now, I freely give of myself because I know this is going to help this doctor out, it will help this patient out. It will make somebody's life better.

There were drawbacks for some participants, particularly those with family responsibilities, when the demands of the job to which they were committed caused role conflict at home. Nick reported that he left an accounting position for a less satisfying government job because of the stress his former job had caused in his family life:

My wife just had a newborn. Right now, I'd like to be home more than what the accounting firm could offer me. I'd go in most mornings for seven and, if I got out at nine o'clock at night, it was a good day. That was for six months of the year; those months were very hard on my wife. I wasn't around as much as I should have been. So we had to prioritize what was important.

Another drawback for some who used a committing strategy was that it gave them a false sense of security. This was the case for Galen. He had been working for five years as an auto parts materials manager when, to his disbelief, he was laid off:

I'd worked hard for the company and thought I'd found a career where I could stick and move up the ladder. I was totally stunned when they laid me off. I knew things were tough for the car companies, but I never thought it would mean losing my job.

Case Study—Committing

Shawn, a 29-year-old chartered accountant from Prince Edward Island, found work that provided him with great satisfaction.

Mostly my work involves auditing, but it can involve some taxation, other special work, dealing with clients. I really enjoy it. You don't see the same thing day after day: you don't know what you're going to be doing when you come in the morning. It can change minute to minute. I like that the most.

Coming out of high school, Shawn didn't know that he wanted to be an accountant. Rather than go straight into a post-secondary program, like most of his friends, Shawn opted to give himself time to think and explore. He described the exploration process which he engaged in:

I wasn't entirely sure what I wanted to do and, for the first while, I was just working at a restaurant, basically to kill time and try to figure out what I did want to do.

After I graduated, I went back [to high school] for another accounting and a calculus course because I liked math. I excelled at it when I was in high school, so I figured that's what I might want to do. I used that as a diving board, just to see if that's what I really wanted to do.

I really did enjoy accounting. My brother had taken an accounting course at college and he had described what it was like to me. I thought maybe that was something I would like to try. I thought college would be a good option because it was low cost as compared to university.

As part of the college program, they had on-the-job training. I went to a small accounting firm to assist. He asked me to come back again the next year so I went back, working full time during the busy season. After a few years, I got inspired and said, "I'm enjoying this, why don't I go the whole way." I decided I'm going to university with the goal of becoming a CA. That's what led me to where I am now.

Analysis: One of the main reasons that Shawn found satisfying work is that he took the time to explore before navigating in a specific direction. Many participants felt pressure to go immediately to college or university, despite being unclear about what they wanted to study.

Shawn's case is a good example of how satisfying decisions come about as a result of incremental exploratory steps that progressively uncover and/or confirm one's interests and abilities and gradually sharpen one's focus to committing to a choice.

- With his parent's *support*, Shawn allowed himself a work *time out* after high school to figure out what he wanted to do.
- He was *aware* that he had an interest and ability in math, so he used that as the starting point.
- By upgrading his high school accounting and math skills, he was able to *confirm* these truly were areas of interest and competency.
- Through his brother, Shawn had access to *reliable information* on what college accounting courses would be like.
- He continued to *test the waters* by starting with a lower-cost college option that included a work

CHAPTER TWO 25

practicum which strengthened his convictions that he had chosen well.

- When full-time work *validated* the depth of his interest, he enrolled in a university program that gave him professional credentialing.

Shawn married and became a parent when he was twenty-three and in third year university. When asked if *marriage* and *parenthood* had any impact on his career path, he said it hadn't because he was already in the process of becoming a chartered accountant when he took on these responsibilities.

If Shawn had been navigating toward a goal that had ended up not being a good fit, he may very well have been forced to stick with that choice in order to support his family. Exploring before navigating increased the chances of him finding satisfying work that he could commit to, rather than having to settle for something that wasn't.

Is One Strategy Better Than Another?

It's easy to assume that navigating is the best strategy to find a career-related place and that committing to is better than settling for a place once it's found. At an age when many were still trying to figure out what to do, Kristen navigated directly from high school into a well-paying job that she loved. Surely, we may reason, it makes sense to encourage all young people to know what they want to do coming out of high school and then to follow through on their plans.

While navigating appears to place young people "ahead" of the game, it doesn't always work out that way. Illustrative of this were the journeys taken by Sophie and Baptiste, who graduated from high school together. Sophie navigated directly to university with the plan of becoming an architect. Baptiste didn't know what he wanted to do and drifted into a job at a fast food restaurant.

Likely those around them at the time were more heartened by Sophie's navigating strategy than Baptiste's drifting. However, ten years later, Baptiste was working in a field that he loved, while Sophie was still trying to figure it out.

Baptiste didn't remain drifting. He joined the army reserves and realized that the military was something that appealed to him. Three years after leaving high school, he started university with the hopes of eventually working in military intelligence. Upon graduation, he was able to join the regular forces as an intelligence officer.

In contrast, Sophie knew very little about being an architect and, two years into her studies, she realized that it wasn't something she wanted to do. She dropped out of school to explore her new-found passion for music.

Eventually, she realized that sound engineering would allow her to make a decent living in the music industry. While she wanted to navigate in that direction, the debt she accumulated pursuing her architect goal put further training out of the question. She was forced to explore music industry options which didn't require her to go back to school.

Navigating, exploring, or drifting

Those participants who did what was expected of them and navigated to a choice without knowing much about its realities were, paradoxically, putting themselves at risk of poor outcomes. In particular, they risked amassing large debts navigating to the wrong program or acquiring credentials for an occupation that they eventually discovered wasn't satisfying.

Those who used an exploring strategy faced a different paradox. Although they were engaged in activities that were developmentally appropriate, they were often criticized because their lack of a career plan ran counter to the Career Myth.

The criticism that young people face when using an exploring strategy is unfortunate because exploring fosters the identity exploration and career production that is central to young people finding satisfying work and building a strong sense of themselves. Moreover, exploring promotes flexible thinking that allows young people to respond more effectively to changing circumstances.

Ideally, exploring would be the primary strategy that young people use in the immediate years after high school. It's hard to choose a career direction until you know yourself well enough to be able to determine what you want. In the best of all worlds, young people would have the opportunity to learn about their interests and abilities and to explore different options before they are required to decide what they are navigating toward.

By the time they graduate from high school, some young people do have enough self-awareness and exposure to occupations to be reasonably confident that what they're navigating towards will be a good fit. Others need more time.

While the proactivity of exploring is generally preferable to the passivity of drifting, drifting does allow for the serendipity of discovering that one's interests and abilities lay in a completely unexpected area. This suggests that it might be advantageous to promote some degree of drifting while young people are exploring. That is, drifting in the sense of trying out new things to see if it might unearth interests, abilities, or opportunities that might otherwise remain undiscovered.

Committing or settling

Finding a career that one can commit to certainly seems to be better than settling for something one's indifferent to. However, it's necessary to look at the larger picture to clearly see the benefits and drawbacks of these two strategies. A lot depends on a person's work orientation, which refers to a person's relationship with work: whether one considers work to be a job, a career, or a calling.[2]

Those who see work primarily as a job value the pay they earn over the work itself. Providing the pay is acceptable and the work is tolerable, they are prepared to settle if the job allows them to do other things outside of their work lives that are personally meaningful. People with a career orientation are also prepared to settle for work they don't find particularly interesting, providing their jobs give them the opportunity to climb the ladder.

Those with a calling orientation don't settle so easily. Pay or prestige may (or may not) come later, but what's most important to them is deriving purpose and satisfaction from the work they do right now. As some participants said, they weren't prepared to either commit to or settle for jobs they didn't find meaningful. For them, the search for fulfillment seemed to be more complex and circuitous. As Kate said, "It's going to be the death of me, I swear, the never-ending quest for meaning in work."

Work orientations aren't quite this straightforward as sometimes people have their feet planted in two camps. They struggle between safeguarding job security and finding meaningful work. Sometimes they feel they should leave their stable, well-paying jobs to follow their passions. They can't, however, bring themselves to give up the security and they tend to remain settled. Anthony shared the internal conflict he was experiencing:

I have an awful lot of security. That's part of the reason why I don't feel that comfortable dropping all of this and going to get my degree in archeology or marine biology. But, every day I look at what's going on in the papers. When they made that discovery off the Atlantic Shelf and they found all these new creatures, I definitely felt a pang of regret. It was like, "I could have been doing that research."

Chapter Three
The Impact of Internal Factors

You have to have a foreshadowing of anything you could ever want to do when you're 18. How do you do that?
∽ Tyrone, 23-year-old from Halifax

When finding a career-related place, study participants didn't intentionally choose one of the strategies discussed in the previous chapter. Instead, a strategy tended to emerge from a convergence of influencing factors that included both internal factors—such as knowing what they wanted, tolerance for ambiguity, and resistance skills—and external factors—such as the messages they received about what they should do, the supports they could access, and the employment opportunities that were available to them.

This chapter focuses on internal factors, while Chapter Four deals with external factors. For the sake of clarity, each factor is discussed separately. In reality, the study found that they interacted with one another in complex and unpredictable ways. While they had an effect on all participants in some way, the degree to which the factors impacted the strategy they used was unique to the individual.

It was also difficult, at times, to distinguish between internal and external factors. For example, knowing what they wanted was impacted by the information and guidance participants received from professionals and non-professionals. Similarly, employment opportunities were strongly influenced by the educational credentials participants possessed.

Knowing What They Wanted

Some participants had clear ideas about what they wanted to do after high school graduation. Nora was one of them. From the time she was in high school, Nora knew she wanted to be a psychologist. In the process of completing a master's degree in counselling psychology, she spoke about how she became aware of her budding abilities:

Mainly it came from the fact that all of my friends came to me for advice and they were always telling me that I was good at it. I've always been a bit of a perfectionist, so I like doing things that I'm considered good at.

Others didn't have specific career goals in mind when they graduated from high school, but they had particular interests or skills they wanted to pursue. Lindsey described her sense of direction when she graduated:

I wanted to have a family and be a mom, for sure. I also knew that I wanted to have a career and I wanted it to involve helping people, working with people, something to do with medicine/health. Other than that, I really had no idea.

Some had no idea what they wanted to do and hadn't spent much time thinking about it. Ravi started university, but left after one semester because he didn't know why he was there. He spoke about needing to take a time-out to widen his horizons:

For me, it was figuring out what I wanted to do and what was important in my life. I had never taken time to think about that stuff, ever. The only time I really thought about it was outside of school when I really wasn't doing too much.

In some cases, participants proclaimed career goals they knew little about. This was the case for Jake who enrolled in software engineering, mainly because he liked computers and his father and sister were engineers. Once graduated, Jake admitted that the work realities of the occupation were completely different from what he'd imagined.

A number of sub-factors seemed to influence the degree to which participants knew what they wanted to do. These included self-awareness, exposure to a range of options, and information and guidance from professionals and non-professionals.

Self-awareness

Some participants had a good sense of their interests, values, and abilities, but many didn't. The stories they told about graduating from high school frequently started with some version of, "I didn't have a clue."

For most participants, self-awareness grew over time as they were exposed to a variety of education, work, and other experiences. Colin captured how his self-awareness had grown through different experiences in the hotel industry:

If you had asked me when I was 20 what I wanted to be, I think I would have felt shameful saying, "I want to run hotels" or "I want to create beautiful experiences for people" or "I want to make people feel good." I think that would have been too fluffy for me to say, but that's what I've always wanted to do. I think I would have just said I want to be a nurse.

Exposure to a range of options

Participants who found a place where they felt satisfied career-wise often credited exposure to a range of educational and occupational experiences for helping them figure out where their interests and abilities lay, and what they did and didn't want to do.

Exposure occurred in a number of ways including high school and/or post-secondary courses, work practicums, paid employment, volunteer experiences, extracurricular activities, and through contact with people who were engaged in a variety of undertakings. It also included being exposed vicariously through observing and listening to the experiences of family members and friends.

Julie thought she might be interested in a social work career, so she used volunteer work experiences to try out various aspects of the profession:

I started at the women's centre two years ago and I volunteered for the after-school program while I was in university. I started at the food bank in January and I've been volunteering with my research project as well. I chose things purposely that I was going to enjoy or thought I was going to enjoy. I wasn't sure I wanted to work with kids in the beginning, but now I love it and I want it to be part of my life. And working with women has always been an interest of mine.

Ben, who owned a marketing business, shared how he became aware of his interest in becoming an entrepreneur:

I've always liked business and I started with an entrepreneurship class in high school. One of our field trips was to a business enterprise centre. I love that place. The government had something they called the Summer Company Program. I went through that just to see if I would really like to get into business. I loved it, loved being my own boss.

Kate, a trained counsellor, described the experience that changed her mind about pursuing veterinary medicine. She loved animals, but quickly realized that taking care of badly injured pets was not for her:

I decided at a very young age that I was going to be a veterinarian. I worked for a vet for a while when I was in high school and it was just a train wreck. It was a good way to determine I didn't want to do it.

Will switched his focus twice, through exposure to one course and a rewarding work experience. After high school, Will planned to go into marketing, so he enrolled in a university business program. In his third year, he took a business policy and law course that tweaked his interest.

CHAPTER THREE 31

Rachelle chanced upon an unexpected new career option through the convergence of two flukes: making a new friend and being in a right time-right place situation:

I went to university and picked the subject that was all wrong for me. But, if I hadn't picked engineering, I would have never ended up as a chef on a yacht. The friend who got me the job was a friend that I met in engineering.

What happened was, the head chef was not getting along with anyone that they put in to be second chef. I'd been working on board for eight months; they knew that I got along with him quite well. It was more important to find someone to get along with him than it was to find somebody with the experience because he could train somebody. That's what I volunteered to do.

Capitalizing on her lucky break, Rachelle began exploring the possibility of starting her own specialty cake business, catering to clientele like the ones she served on the yacht.

Socioeconomic status seemed to play a role in what participants were exposed to as they matured. Those from middle-class families seemed more likely to have taken music lessons, been enrolled in sports programs, travelled, and attended university than those who grew up in working-class families. Where participants grew up—in big city or small town/rural community—influenced the range of

He subsequently enrolled in law school, with the intention of becoming a corporate lawyer. When he was turned down for a clerkship with a corporate law firm, he went to work with a firm representing plaintiffs in class action suits. The satisfaction he got from making a difference in clients' lives redirected his interests to becoming a class action lawyer.

Exposure to an occupation helped some participants discover or verify not just their interests, but other aspects of their identity. Misha imagined herself working on public service campaigns when she landed an advertising agency job. Instead, she found her values being challenged when she was assigned to a plastic surgery clinic account: "I ended up hawking fake boobs and vaginal reconstruction. I realized that a lot of that career would be convincing people to buy stuff I didn't think they needed."

An element of serendipity was frequently present in the career exposure experiences of participants. They often mentioned that the way they discovered an education program or occupation was through a friend or family member's casual comment. Several spoke of "falling into" jobs that ended up being what they wanted to do.

Anna, an environmental scientist, related such a chance event in her student life. Her original plan had been to specialize in emergency medicine. In her second year, she was dreading taking a required ecology course because of the professor's reputation. Luckily, that professor was on sabbatical leave and a dynamic replacement brought ecology to life for her. It was doubtful she would have switched programs if it hadn't been for this fortunate happenstance.

people they encountered and the breadth of occupational diversity to which they were exposed. Jordan reflected on the limitations of his occupational exposure when he was growing up:

If I had grown up in Halifax, I think I'd have a broader view of opportunities. Living in PEI, you look at things inside the box as far as what's available. When I was graduating from high school, it was like, "The computer industry is booming right now, I'm going to take that." In Halifax, there's just so many more things like social work or occupational therapy. I didn't even know what an occupational therapist was until my aunt got her degree in it. I was so naïve about certain opportunities.

While knowledge about an option increased the likelihood that it would be suitable, it wasn't a guarantee. A number of participants had been exposed to an education program or occupation before starting it, but discovered later that it wasn't what they'd imagined or the job market in their specialty was flat when they graduated. Bonita, a human service worker, took an office administration program immediately after graduating from high school:

My family comes from a strong background in business and I felt this is what I'd really like to do. It turned out, when I finished, I didn't want what I had chosen. I'm not a person to sit behind a desk. I don't mind it, but I want to be out there, actually hands on, helping people because that's who I really am.

Information and guidance from professionals

The majority of participants recounted stories of making post-secondary and occupational decisions knowing very little about what they had chosen or any alternatives. Few received occupation-related information or career guidance from a counsellor, either in high school or at the post-secondary level.

Participants spoke about how their academic performance in high school "pigeonholed" them when it came to examining post-secondary options with guidance counsellors. It was assumed that, if they were "good students" in high school, they would go to university. Participants who were labelled "poor" students said that they were expected to go to college or directly into the workforce. As a result, the good students were typically not given information about colleges or the trades. Poor-performing students weren't given information about universities and, sometimes, weren't given any information at all.

Perry described how high school course selection labelled him and his friend and impacted the guidance they received regarding post-secondary options:

At that time, if you went into the [pre-calculus] math class, then you were automatically supposed to go to university. There was no talk of trades or any other avenues at all. It was all "this is the way to go." I remember we had to choose a math course. It was either [my friend] was going to choose the academic math, or we used to call it "dummy math," one plus one kind of stuff.

He chose to take that one and I was like, "Why would you do that?" and he was like, "I just don't like it, I don't care, I know I can do the other, but I don't care."

Then he took a free instead of taking French or gym class. So he took the bare bones and, of course, they told him to go to trade school. He took welding, or whatever, and dropped out. Now he's got a psychology degree and he's working with at-risk youth.

Ironically, Perry's friend was encouraged to go into the trades for which he had no interest, while Perry was encouraged to go to university even though he preferred hands-on learning.

Those who went to university sometimes talked to individual professors about future career goals. Not surprisingly, the information they received tended to be confined to the professor's subject area and the most common topic discussed concerned graduate school. Participants who attended college received more assistance from their instructors, most typically around the employment prospects associated with their training.

Several participants indicated that, when they entered post-secondary education, their plans were already in place, so they didn't bother seeing a counsellor. After graduation, when their plans didn't materialize, they were no longer eligible to access counselling services or, at least, they didn't know how to do so. This was also true for those participants who didn't attend post-secondary education who wanted advice after they left high school, but didn't know how to approach their former guidance counsellor.

Vanessa said that she didn't seek out guidance while she was in high school or university because her pre-made plan was to go into medical school. When that didn't work out, she had no idea what else to do:

I needed someone to help me in the right direction. Maybe that's why I did my travelling and working at different types of jobs for as long as I did. My family couldn't guide me and say, "You're really good at this, why don't you go back to school and do this?" Not to put blame on them. It's just they didn't really have the knowledge. Not having that, I needed to go off and find out who I was.

The few participants who received career guidance from a professional had mixed reviews on their experiences. Most of them said that they found it helpful when counsellors explored with them whether their burgeoning ideas were a good match with their interests and abilities, or pointed them in the direction of a promising alternative.

Galen described how his experience with the guidance counsellor helped him discover a route to the field of materials management:

In my last year at high school I didn't really know what I wanted to do. I became interested in business administration. I went through some tests and my guidance counsellor was able to see the sort of things that I was interested in.

She had a student the year before who had gone to this program and they really liked the program. It was a match with some of my interests and so she recommended it to me.

I didn't just go ahead and jump into it. I went to a couple of open houses at the college and got a feel for it. I was really interested and decided to pursue it.

It's unlikely that Galen would have been able to navigate so directly to a suitable training program without someone helping him to translate his interests and make the connection with an appropriate career goal.

By contrast, Julie's take on her interaction with a counsellor was anything but helpful in generating possible options that she might start to explore. She spoke about her frustrations:

My guidance counsellor was zero help. There was just a lack of information. She would be like, "What are your interests?" You'd tell her and she'd be like, "Have you thought what you could do with those interests?" Not giving options, but asking me what the options are. I don't know. That's why I'm coming to the guidance counsellor.

Information and advice from non-professionals

Participants cited non-professionals such as family members, friends, and employers as being beneficial sources of practical information and advice.

Not surprisingly, parents who attended college or university were able to provide their children with more guidance about post-secondary education than those who hadn't. Ravi recounted how his mother helped him research different educational programs: "I remember my mom getting the Dalhousie calendar. She would read about different courses and really help me figure out what sounded interesting to me."

In a number of cases, friends and older siblings were credited with being important sources of information regarding post-secondary options, occupations, and job opportunities. Occasionally, employers were mentioned as providing valuable mentorship opportunities.

Despite the information and advice offered, few participants received explicit career advice from non-professionals beyond, "Do what makes you happy." Vanessa assessed the value of this well-intentioned, but simplistic, counsel:

My parents were so intent on not biasing my opinions about where to go and what to do. They would always say, "Do what you're interested in." But I never really knew what I was interested in. I would have appreciated a sit-down and they would help me explore the options. I guess maybe they didn't know about the options.

A number of participants said that the information they received from friends, family, and employers at a critical juncture helped them to move along the course they had set or begin exploring in new directions. Jeremy, a youth minister, described how his friends' advice helped him to clarify his thoughts and start exploring options that were more compatible with his interests than his original choice had been:

I started off in chemistry and was doing well at it. But I woke up one night in a cold sweat, thinking that I was going to be a chemist for the rest of my life. I thought I was locked into this program.

I was relaying this story to somebody and they're like, "Why don't you just switch programs?" It's like, "You

I'm taking music. That probably means what I'm going to do. I'm a musician." I did what I wanted to do. That was one lucky thing I had that very few of my friends had: actually knowing what I wanted to do.

All of the participants in the study who used the exploring strategy had at least some sense of their interests, values, or skills. Hannah became aware of human rights and community development through volunteer work she did in high school. That experience resonated with her interests and values and propelled her to participate in an international educational exchange program after graduating:

After high school, I didn't really have a clear idea what I wanted to do. I knew that I wanted to travel, experience other cultures. I knew that I wanted to make a difference. I knew that I wanted to work with people in some context.

A lot of the focus [of the Canada World Youth program] was around cross-cultural learning, community development, leadership development. I was just manifesting all of those desires and passions and skills. I think that first step led to the next thing and led to the next thing. Here I am now, with a great job working with youth from cross-cultural backgrounds.

Because Hannah had some perception of her interests and values, she was able to recognize the Canada World Youth program as something that would be in harmony with her growing self-awareness. Participating in the program

can do that?" Another friend suggested religious studies and I was thinking about music. So I went and found the information about all those programs.

Impact on strategy utilization

Those participants who had been exposed to a wider range of options and had received information and guidance from professionals and non-professionals seemed to have a fuller appreciation of who they were and what types of education programs or career possibilities might be a good fit. They tended to have better frames of reference for evaluating promising options and for making more informed decisions.

They also seemed more likely to explore or navigate toward post-secondary education programs or jobs that were congruent with their personal attributes—providing external factors didn't hamper their pursuits. For example, in order to navigate or explore, participants also needed supportive messages or the resistance skills to ignore critical ones. They may also have needed financial support and a receptive labour market to successfully achieve their goals.

Andy, a professional musician, personified how knowing what he wanted allowed him to navigate directly to his chosen field:

As soon as I realized music was my thing, I had no other option. It just wouldn't make sense to do anything else. I figured that out in grade 11. When I started thinking about university, then I was like, "Of course,

confirmed her interests and values which, in turn, led her to seek out other education and work opportunities that allowed her to further express her identity.

Participants who didn't have this "internal compass" to guide them were inclined to use a drifting strategy. Some drifted from one experience to another in an attempt to learn more about themselves. Vanessa explained that her lack of self-awareness left her adrift when her application to medical school was declined:

This was way too much, too fast. My counter-approach was to work in industries like the restaurant industry and at department stores because it was this whole breath of fresh air. "Like, people do this? People just go out and work at Eaton's and I can do this?" I felt that, somehow, I was gaining control of discovering who I was, trying to figure more out about me.

For some, not knowing what they wanted caused them to settle. They hadn't discovered a career field that caught their interest, so they continued in a job that was unfulfilling. Elizabeth shared the experience of a friend who had settled:

I have a friend who took a communications certificate and is doing PR work for a big company. She doesn't hate it, but doesn't really like it either. I think she's staying because she's not sure what else she wants to do.

Tolerance for Ambiguity

Whether participants navigated, explored, or drifted into post-secondary education programs or jobs, there were often many alterations along the way. As a result, most participants experienced at least some uncertainty about their career journeys during the school-to-work transition. Scott described the doubts he had experienced since graduating from high school:

Uncertainty and I are close friends. I was so uncertain for three years. Uncertain that what I was doing was the right thing, uncertain that I could make it work, uncertain if I tried something else would I fail and end up back where I was, uncertain I was going to be able to pay the bills on time. You know, character building, but not very comfortable.

Some participants were comfortable with this ambiguity, while others weren't. Colin talked about how upsetting it was if things didn't go his way:

I want plans even if none of them come through. I want to know as much as I can about what I'm going into. If things don't go my way, forget about it. It's over. If things go exactly the way I want, which they often do because I set them up that way, I'm really happy. But, if things don't, I'm pissed.

Those who were able to tolerate uncertainty were typically optimistic about their future. Carol exemplified this confidence when she said that, despite not knowing what her future held, whatever happened she had faith that it "will take me somewhere great."

Participants' optimism often seemed to be connected to trusting their feelings or something outside of themselves. Emma said that, when she moved home to weigh her options rather than going to graduate school, she was sure that it was the right thing to do:

I really trust my intuition about things. I feel like I should be living here for some reason. I can't tell you why, but I feel like there's something, something's going to happen.

Others thought there was someone or something guiding them. Some felt this guidance came from a spiritual source; others couldn't specify its origins. Andy explained that his meditation practice helped him work through the "fundamental groundlessness of my situation." Lindsey said:

There's been periods of time where I have felt very confused and have no idea where I'm going. Then, all of a sudden, something comes to me. It feels like there's somebody just handing things to me.

Several participants said that, over time, they had learned to be less anxious in the face of the unknown. Torin recounted how his tolerance for ambiguity quotient had grown:

I thought I knew what I wanted to do and then things fell apart. I found something else to do and it fell apart. Over time, I've become more comfortable with uncertainty. Experience has taught me that something will fall into my lap. So I think, "Okay, I'll take things as they come." The past couple of years, things have worked out without a plan.

Impact on strategy utilization

A tolerance for ambiguity helped some participants navigate toward careers that were inherently uncertain, such as being an entrepreneur or artist, because they felt strongly that this was the place they were meant to be. Others who could tolerate uncertainty were able to leave situations that weren't suitable and navigate toward ones that were. Jeremy discussed the internal struggle he went through in weighing job security against finding something more personally meaningful:

When I decided that religious studies was the thing that I wanted to do rather than chemistry, there was a big question for me about security. "Do I take chemistry where I know I'm going to have security? Do I take this path of the unknown, not knowing what I'm going to do?" That's when I made the decision that following what I want to do is more important than security.

Some participants who weren't as comfortable also navigated—but for different reasons. Those who felt vulnerable not being in control seemed to be more inclined to rush into taking action—any action— because it gave them a sense that they were moving forward. This was apparent in participants who enrolled in programs they didn't know much about or weren't particularly interested in. It was even seen in participants, like Nora, who moved onward to advanced degree programs.

Nora's plan was to complete a master's degree in clinical psychology immediately after her undergraduate work. When her application was declined, she was so at loose ends that, the following year, she applied to four different psychology programs, including one in experimental psychology, for which she had no interest. When asked if she would have taken that program if she hadn't been accepted into any other, she said:

After not getting into a grad program that first time, there was no way I was taking the chance of not being in school. Getting into any program was better than not being in school.

Often participants with a low tolerance for ambiguity were loath to give up on a plan that was already in play, even when they discovered it wasn't a good fit. They were more likely to continue navigating toward that option or they would find another closely-related option and start navigating toward that.

Being able to accept ambiguity seemed to facilitate exploring, which is not surprising since exploring is intrinsically uncertain. For others, like Nora, being insecure about the unfamiliar circumscribed the options they were prepared to explore:

I never thought of something that would be out of the box because being a doctor or lawyer is a good career. There's job security in that. I would love to be a wedding planner, but most small businesses fail and just how do you start that? How do you become one? That kind of thing would have scared me. I had to be in the box. Like, there's a career for what I want. I don't need to figure out how to become a psychologist. There's degrees out there.

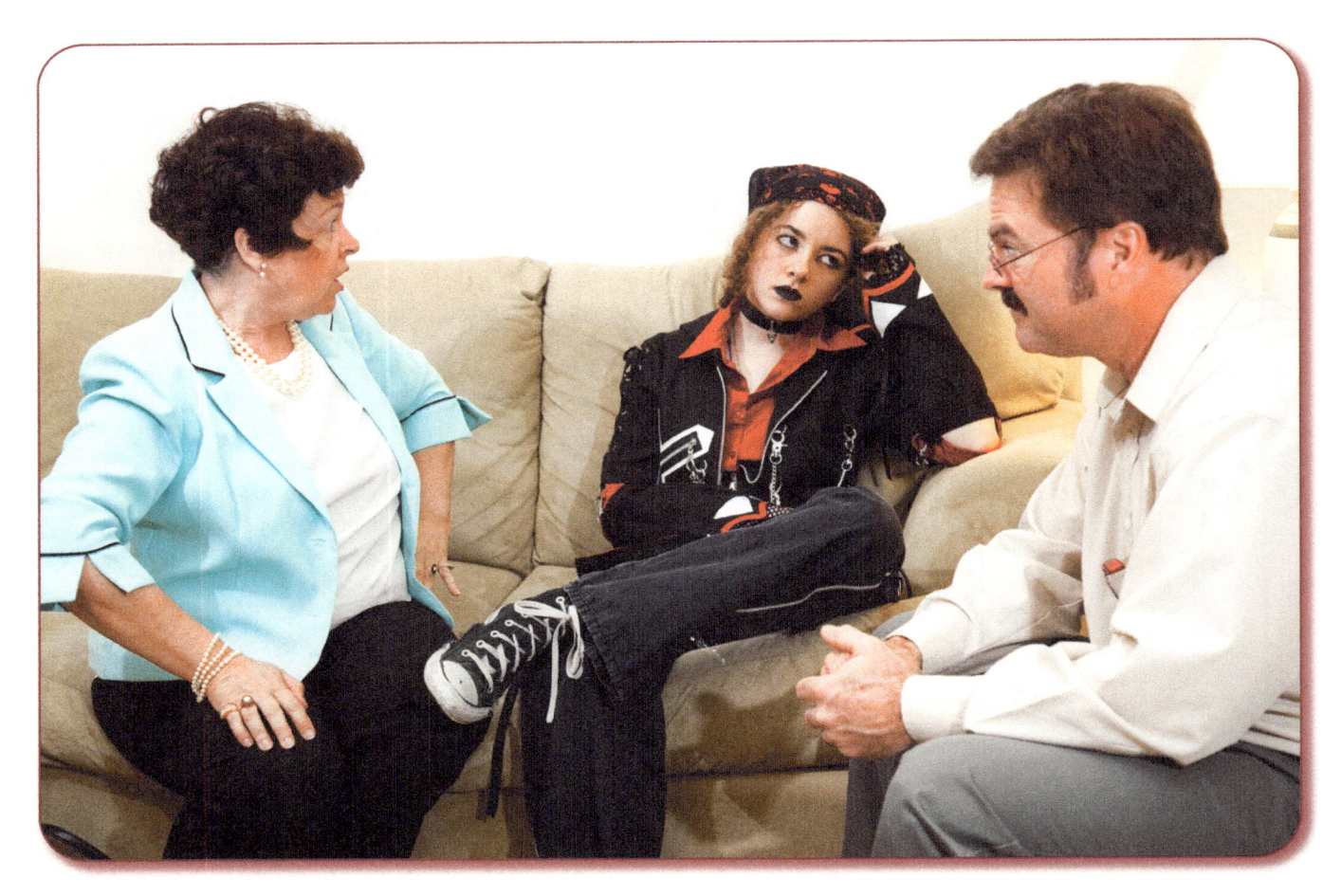

For some participants, like Torin, a tolerance for uncertainty allowed them to handle set-backs and not rush into making snap decisions. Having recently learned that he wasn't accepted into medical school, Torin said that he was going to allow himself the opportunity to explore other avenues of interest. He admitted that, had he been in the same situation a few years earlier, he would have been so uneasy not knowing what was going to happen that he would have been "desperately searching for a career."

Some participants chose to drift for fear of making the wrong decision or when they weren't accepted into their program of choice. Stacey reflected on why she drifted after high school:

I remember graduating and thinking, "I don't want to deal with school." Work was a way of being lazy because all you've got to do is show up, do your job, and go home. There's nothing stressful or uncertain about it, whereas applying to school and making choices about your future, it's scary.

Resistance Skills

The concept of resistance skills comes from the positive youth development literature which uses the term to refer to a young person's ability to resist negative patterns of behaviour, like drug abuse or delinquency, in order to fit in with a peer group.[1] In the context of this study, resistance skills are defined as a young person's ability to challenge the expectations of significant others (peers, parents, and the community) when those expectations are in conflict with what the person wants to do him or herself.

Participants varied in their abilities to withstand powerful messages as they navigated their way into and through post-secondary education and then moved into the workforce. Some were able to resist the expectations of others and pursued options they thought would be personally satisfying. Some took the path of least resistance by passively doing what was expected of them or making choices that were closest at hand. Still others took time off to figure out what they wanted to do.

While it was never easy, a few had developed resistance skills by their late teens; for others, these skills grew as they progressed through their twenties. Kate was an aspiring actress who suffered her in-laws' cutting remarks about selling "candlelight products for the rest of your life." She capitulated to their repeated reproofs to find a "real job" and spent two "miserable" years working as a government administrative assistant. Along the way, her resistance skills began to germinate:

A little voice inside me started to grow: "These people don't have it all together. They don't know what the hell they're doing either. Everyone's making it up. So, I might as well make it up in a way that is going to honour certain drives and needs that are mine."

One of the most common techniques participants used to resist critical messages was to strategically control the flow of information. They often changed their plans without telling others and only told them once the alternative plan was in place. Another favoured technique was to enlist the support of family members, friends, and others who encouraged them to follow their desires.

Impact on strategy utilization

The ability to resist the expectations of others was critical for participants whose goals weren't compatible with the people who were significant in their lives. It gave some the courage to buck the pressures of staying in programs that didn't fit or "good jobs" that weren't satisfying.

Lindsey described leaving a college program she didn't like despite pressure from her parents and friends to stick it out to the end:

I knew it didn't fit and I didn't want to stay. But it was hard telling my parents and people around me, "I'm quitting." They're like, "No, just finish. It's only a year; just do it." But I was like, "If I'm stuck here for a year, it's not going to make me happy." If I hadn't left, I wouldn't have done the HR jobs. I think it worked out personally, but definitely then it was, "If I quit, I'm a failure and, if I stay, I'm going to be unhappy." It was a good choice, but it was a hard choice, for sure.

Dylan, a successful hair stylist, went along with his parents' wishes—up to a point. Hairdressing had been Dylan's dream when he graduated from high school. His parents, however, wanted him to go to university. He completed his undergraduate degree to "pacify" them, but held firm when they pushed him to continue pursuing graduate work:

My father was a foreman; he didn't want me having a trade. He wanted me to have an education. The scariest thing ever is to go against my parents' wishes. I think I whispered to my aunt, this is what I wanted to do, and she encouraged me. Then she got hold of my older sister and we were able to keep it low and not tell anyone.

I wasn't happy for four years at university. I felt like I was treading water and not going anywhere. But, as soon as I was done university and able to take a course that I wanted to take, that was the best part.

Initially, Dylan didn't have the resistance skills to withstand his father's wishes. Over time, these skills grew and he was able to navigate in the direction he wanted. When asked where he might be if he hadn't been able to resist his parents' expectations, Dylan said he likely would have settled for a civil servant job: "I would have been in Ottawa somewhere, probably pushing papers or having a boring life."

Resistance skills were often needed by participants in order for them to employ exploring or drifting strategies, particularly when they occurred outside of post-secondary education. Many participants said that they would have liked to have taken time off before or after going to university or college. They didn't, however, have the fortitude to stand up to the message that they should enrol in post-secondary immediately after high school or get a "real" job after graduating.

Some participants had "real" jobs, ones that paid well and had a secure future. When they began to doubt the soundness of their career decision, they found it particularly difficult to take time out to figure out what they really wanted to do. Ethan, an engineer, spoke about his decision to leave his job of two years:

It's a hell of a lot easier to just stay at a job, keep making money, and just keep it going. It's a lot harder to take that leap and say, "No, I've gotta do something else," or "I gotta go figure it out." Yeah, it's definitely not easy.

Some participants who weren't able to stand up to the messages they were hearing opted to settle. Jenna explained what kept her in a job she didn't like for two years:

My parents were really excited about this job. They were saying, "You could stay there for life. You could make this a career. You could move up." But I knew that it wasn't for me and I would hate my life.

Chapter Four

The Impact of External Factors

It's been a big lesson in life that things don't work out the way you envision. You're not always in charge.
— Bartley, a 27-year-old from Prince Edward Island

The previous chapter discussed the internal factors that impacted the strategies that participants used to progress on their career journeys. In this chapter, the external factors are explored.

Messages

Participants were bombarded with strong messages—both spoken and implied—about what was acceptable and expected in their education and career choices. Four messages surfaced as being the most pervasive: Go to university or college. You need to have a plan. Changing your mind is not a good thing. Some choices are better than others.

Go to university or college. This was the most common message that participants heard after high school. Even those who didn't proceed onto post-secondary education felt that they should at some point.

Many said that post-secondary education wasn't really a choice: it was assumed to be the next step. Moreover, it was implied that university was the superior option to college and that, if the young person was capable, university should be their choice.

Will explained what was expected of him after graduating from high school:

If you're smart enough, you should go to university and that's how it was presented. If not, you should go to college to learn a skill. Then there's this terrible shame of not doing either and just working. Like, that was not acceptable or that you should be striving for more.

It's important to note that this expectation was less prevalent among participants whose parents didn't attend post-secondary themselves and among participants who hadn't done well academically in high school.

You need to have a plan. For most, going to post-secondary education stood as a proxy for having a plan. Some viewed it as an avenue to explore their options and they were given the message that they "would figure it out." After graduation, the message changed to, "It's time to make up your mind." As Jeff said:

After university, people start asking you, "What are you going to do? What are you going to do? What are you going to do?" That just puts pressure on people to quickly decide and not get to know themselves well enough to make an informative decision.

Changing your mind is not a good thing. Some participants felt that they should complete whatever post-secondary program they had started, whether they liked it or not. This was the case for Chris:

When I went to university you had to pick something, so I picked computer science. When I had doubts about it, I thought, "I'm already so far. How can I start over again?" Even when I was going to grad school in computer science, I thought, "Maybe I want to do something else." But it always seemed so difficult to change once you were committed. It may have been completely in my head, but it never felt easy.

Even when participants did decide to change their plans, it wasn't easy. Often their strategy was to develop another plan before telling their parents. When Bianca realized she had made a mistake enrolling in an early childhood program, she went through a period of panicked confusion:

I thought, "Crap, why did I make this decision? What do I do? Do I finish the program? Do I drop out?" When the job opportunity came up, it was, "I can drop out of the program and that will be okay with my parents."

Some choices are better than others. Many heard that they should have "good" jobs and "stable" jobs. Parents who were professionals themselves often expected their children to follow suit. Jake said that the only occupations that were acceptable to his parents were doctor, lawyer, or engineer. Adam said, "I told my mother I wanted to be a mechanic when I was in grade 8 or grade 9 and she cried."

Parents who weren't professionals seemed to be more accepting of their children considering occupations that didn't have as much status. Jason, whose father was a factory worker, said his parents were fine with him going to university, but they also told him, "It doesn't matter what you do. You can work in the factory and, if that's the best you can do for now or if it ends up being the best you can do, then that's fine."

Many participants said that they were encouraged to choose a career that was "stable" and provided "security." Some reported that, while their parents wanted them to have a secure job, they also encouraged them to find occupations that they enjoyed. Torin described the confusion this mixed messaging created for him:

There's pressure put on me to find something stable. I've rejected it and accepted it and gone back and forth with it. I'm definitely struggling with how to balance finding my passion, which they've always been supportive of. That doesn't necessarily jive with being in a profession that's stable.

Participants who wanted to pursue careers in the arts seemed to take the brunt of parents' (and society's) scepticism or outright disapproval. Sophie, an aspiring musician, quipped, "People love music, but they hate musicians."

Those who persevered with their arts and music career goals, despite the criticism, often doubted their decision. Sophie explained that it was a constant struggle to convince herself that her passion for performing was a worthwhile pursuit. Every few months, she would feel that she should be doing something more "productive."

Impact on strategy utilization

The messages that participants heard had a strong influence on which strategies they utilized. Navigating towards an acceptable post-secondary program and/or career choice was the strategy that emerged for many immediately after graduating from high school. Many said that attending college or university was not their choice, but something that was heavily encouraged or even foisted on them. Arif explained how he, like most young people he knew, went to university because that was what was expected:

It's not really their decision to go. It is their decision, they can say no, but the majority of people won't. I didn't. None of my friends did. Your parents want you to go, so you just do it. You're only 17, 18; you're still a kid. You don't even know if you know how to say "no" to your parents.

The fact that it wasn't a personal choice meant that many participants weren't motivated to succeed or were enrolled in a program that wasn't a good fit. Speaking about some of his classmates in his golf management program, Mike said:

Their parents just shoved them in there because they needed to go to school. They dropped out; they didn't care; they didn't get good grades. They had no idea what they wanted to do, and their parents made them choose something.

Messages that promoted or stigmatized an education or occupational choice limited the options that some participants were willing/able to explore. Some were caught in a bind because, as Chris explained, "The things I was naturally interested in weren't okay. The things that were okay didn't interest me."

Some participants drifted because their career aspirations weren't acceptable to those around them. Jeff, an aspiring musician, described what he did to try to placate his family:

I applied to community college, like two or three times. I got in, but I didn't go because I didn't want to. The reason I was applying, I didn't know it at the time, was to pacify my mother because she wanted to see me do something.

Drifting was a strategy that was strongly discouraged, particularly if the young person wanted to do it immediately after high school. The message was, if they didn't continue immediately onto post-secondary education, they may never go.

Many participants said that, rather than embarking on a career choice they weren't sure about, they did, or could have, benefited from a time-out before, during, or after completing post-secondary education. But the opposition they encountered was hard to defy. For those with low resistance skills, drifting into or back into a post-secondary program, whether or not it held any interest, was a common fall-back strategy.

Those who persisted and took a break frequently had to put up with disparaging commentary. Emma, who found her niche in the publishing industry, decided to take a time-out after finishing her bachelor of arts degree. She was feeling pressure to continue with a graduate or professional program, but wasn't sure what direction to take. Emma described how her friends and family reacted when she opted for a work stint in retail instead:

I was literally having people call me and say, "You need to leave; you're wasting your time. I always thought you would amount to something."

My parents, at first: "You're living with us and you don't have any money. You worked really hard and you did well in school, so it's okay. Don't worry about it." But that turned into, "When are you going to pull it together and go back to school?"

They're very supportive but, at the same time, they want me to do well. I think they were very worried that I would suddenly do nothing with my life. So there was a push there.

Some used settling as a coping strategy. Once they started navigating, particularly toward an occupation-specific goal, there was sometimes pressure to stick to the plan and "just finish it off," whether they liked it or not. As a result, several graduated with a credential they didn't want to use. Andy talked about a friend's experience:

She finished her nursing degree and she said, by the time she realized that she did not like that profession, she was in third year and she felt that she had to finish it. She's currently a nurse and she hates every day of it.

Other participants used settling as a way to quiet the question that never seemed to go away. For some who hadn't formulated a plan after graduating from high school or post-secondary education, it was easier to continue with their studies or take a job because that would "answer what I wanted to do with my life." Ainsley, a community studies graduate, opted for a job in a call centre:

The pressure to know what you're going to do with the rest of your life is pretty great. I found that to be almost debilitating because I didn't know and everybody kept asking. I pretty much took the first job that I was offered because I thought, "If I had a job, then that would be the answer."

The urgency of the message to make up your mind and have a plan intensified as participants moved into their mid-to-late twenties. Whether or not they had found something that suited them, many thought it was time to establish a career. As Lyle put it:

A lot of people feel pressured to start something by the time they're 30. They should be doing something that they're settled in; they're in a spot where they can start a family. I think a lot of people want to settle based on societal pressure.

For participants who had committed to their career pathway, there was often congruence between what they wanted and what others expected of them. But, even there, doubts lingered whether they would have been able to withstand the pressure, if the support hadn't been behind them. Shawn, a chartered accountant, pondered that very question: "I'm wondering how well I would have coped if I was made to be a carpenter. I would like to say that I would do what I wanted, but I don't know if that would be the case."

Financial Support

Money factors into young people's educational decisions as never before. Youth know that suitable and sustaining labour market attachment depends on increasing amounts of post-secondary education. They also know that education is getting more and more expensive. For many participants, therefore, the availability of financing determined their choice of education program, institution, and number of years they attended—or whether they attended at all.

Some participants' families were able to pay for all or most of their children's education, but many were not in a position to contribute. In many cases, participants paid most, if not all, of the costs by working and/or taking out student loans.

While taking on student loans was a deterrent for some, it wasn't for most, and many participants incurred significant debt in order to attend post-secondary education. A number of participants weren't sure how their degrees would relate to future employment. For them, mounting student debt was the impetus to leave their program of study before graduation.

Those who financed their own education usually worked while studying, sometimes holding down two or three jobs at the same time. Juggling work and full course loads resulted in lower grades for some which, in turn, limited their ability to enter graduate, professional, or specialized college programs later on.

Impact on strategy utilization

The availability of financial support skewed the strategies that participants employed in several important ways. Some participants would have preferred to navigate toward a chosen occupation or explore an area of interest by attending a post-secondary institution. Because they had no choice but to take on large student debt, some deferred enrolling until they could save enough to cover their expenses. Others opted, or were compelled, to not go at all. A few drifted into the workforce or just drifted.

Anthony, who had a long-standing interest in geology and archaeology, explained why he chose to work instead of going to university:

At the time, I didn't have the funding. That got me started working at Canadian Tire: "I'll work there part time and go to school part time." I never did go to school part time. I really didn't want the overhead of student loans because I'd seen them go horribly wrong. I kept hearing about this person just graduated from university and they owe 20, 30, $40,000.

Often, high levels of student debt also impacted the strategies participants used after graduation. Some felt they had to settle for the best paying jobs, rather than the most interesting ones or the ones that appeared to have long-term potential. Roz described the impact that financing her own education and having to repay $40,000 in student loans had on her budding marketing career:

Finances are probably the biggest barrier because you make your decisions not based on what you think is right, but what you can afford. I may not have gone the corporate route. I may have gone a more social work route, but they didn't pay for their co-ops. So I think finances impact a lot of my decisions.

I've got a second job waitressing now, where I could be taking this great volunteer leadership program with different professionals from the public/private sectors. They come together to do courses on board governance or project management and it's a big network. I'm hopefully going to do this program, but I may have to defer it because, right now, my priority is to pay down some of these loans.

Other indebted participants found it difficult to navigate toward their chosen field because they were unable or unwilling to extend their student loans to continue acquiring the credentials they believed were necessary to get "good jobs." Jenna was unemployed and having difficulty finding satisfying work. She talked about the conundrum she was facing trying to reconcile the goal she wanted to pursue with the financing it would take:

I could totally see myself going back. I would do a master's degree. I would do a PhD. It's just the financials. I had a $30,000 debt I will probably be paying for a long time. It's just not feasible at the moment. But, ideally that's what I'd love to do. I'd probably go back and do the MSW because there's a lot more you could do with it.

Emotional Support

Most participants acknowledged the strong encouragement and emotional support they received from families, partners, and friends. Several cited self-help and "positive mindset" books as important sources of insight and inspiration.

Angie described how having multi-tiered support from her family helped her make it through her first year of university:

I had a terrible roommate. We didn't get along and it really affected everything. From my grades to my outlook, I was ready to drop out; I was ready to come home.

My parents were excellent. They would turn up on a week night, when I was in tears. They would bring me home on weekends. My boyfriend at the time, now husband, would drop everything, turn up at the drop of a hat, and encourage me in any way possible. My brother too: he was one year ahead of me so he'd been through everything before. He was incredibly supportive and helpful.

Several participants talked about how helpful career counsellors had been at helping them find constructive ways to get out of abusive work situations or lifting them up when they were feeling deflated. David described how a career counsellor helped him regain hope that things would get better when he was at a particularly low point:

He was such a positive influence. It was so important because I was working 13 hours a day and my life sucked. I'd go see him and I'd feel like I'm going to get out of this terrible mess because someone believes I can and they are going to show me how. The biggest thing I got out of the process was self-confidence. It made me less afraid of the world and got me to realize, "You went through some bad stuff, but you are still pretty good." It created positivity in me that allowed me to make things happen for myself.

Emotional support can be felt most by its absence. Participants who received scant emotional support because of the death or emotional withdrawal of their parents spoke about having lower self-confidence and lacking the motivation to pursue post-secondary education.

Impact on strategy utilization

Having emotional support helped participants to freely explore their interests and options and then navigate, with greater confidence, toward their chosen goals. For those whose aspirations might have seemed unorthodox or risky, emotional support was even more crucial. Rather than the critical messages experienced by many musicians, Andy said that his family's backing fuelled his music career:

My family and even my grandparents have encouraged me every minute of everything I've ever done. I've never felt any resistance or opposition. It was almost more inspiring than anything. It made me work harder. I never felt like they were pushing me. It was just like, "We're going to support you."

Several participants mentioned that having emotional support from some people countered the impact of critical messages from others and helped them to navigate forward. Jenna was criticized by her father for wanting to navigate away from economics to sociology so that she could pursue a career in the helping professions. She explained what helped her withstand her father's opposition:

The acceptance that I got from the Dean that it was an okay decision to make, to not stick to this. I had been ingrained that hard skills were important and frivolous art courses aren't. They're not for my type of people. He backed me and he's a very powerful, prominent person in the school.

Emotional support was also important for those who experienced roadblocks to navigating, such as not being accepted into their program of choice or having doubts about their abilities. Nora described getting just-in-time reassurance from her professors when her application for graduate school was declined:

The message was, "Keep going, you have what it takes. We don't understand why it didn't happen." It was really encouraging, like keep trying.

In a few cases, family members demonstrated their emotional support by tolerating exploration activities, even if it appeared, at times, to be drifting. Rebecca talked about the support she received:

My friends and family are very open to the idea of wandering through life until something hits you, as long as you can pay your bills and you're happy. I hear things like, "You better find something to do soon," or "Time's ticking." I've never had these pressures.

A lack of emotional support hindered some from navigating toward a career they cherished. Lucy spoke about why her high school dream of becoming an administrative assistant wasn't acted upon:

My mother didn't care. It didn't matter what I did as long as I cleaned the house. Growing up, we weren't allowed to do our homework until the house was cleaned. I would be a professional student all my life, that's how much I like it, but they're not really interested. So no, I didn't get good messages about what to be or where to go in my life.

For some, non-supportive work experiences early in their careers undermined their confidence and impacted their abilities to continue navigating in the direction they had chosen. Taylor had aspired to a career as an art curator. She had been pursuing her dream since high school by working in galleries, first as a weekend assistant and later as part of a university fine arts co-op placement. After graduating, she secured a contract job with an art gallery:

I thought it was my big break. I thought that it was me stepping out of university into my career. It turned out to be an absolute nightmare. My boss was abusive mentally and emotionally. I left five months into my contract and I haven't worked in the field of art since. It was just a really bad start to my career.

I went through a period of being extremely afraid to apply for any jobs in the art world, let alone talk to anybody from the art world. I felt like she probably dragged me through the mud. I've become more involved again, but it definitely had a major impact on my confidence and I think it really affected my aspiring career.

Five years after this demoralizing experience, Taylor was still trying to gain enough self-confidence to make another attempt at the art world.

Colin had a similarly abusive boss, but was able to leave emotionally unscathed because of the support he received from a career counsellor:

I was so scared to quit. I felt I needed her to tell me what to do. We ended up talking about how I could successfully leave my job. I left with advice and skills and a perspective that was very valuable at getting out of a very bad situation in order to move on to something else. I think if it had gone really sour when I left [my job] that it would have destroyed me in a way.

Those who didn't have support to help them resist critical messages seemed more likely to settle for the programs or jobs they had, even if they didn't find them rewarding. Kate said that one of the reasons she succumbed to the messages from her in-laws to stick with a meaningless job was that if she moved away, she would be "cut off from her support system."

Participants' reports of having received a great deal of backing from their parents seemed, at times, to be at odds with their actual experiences of parents threatening to withdraw financial or emotional support if a participant's decision didn't align with theirs. Emma's experience of the conditional nature of her parents' support had a profound influence on the direction she chose to navigate:

I was very interested in photography, in going to NSCAD [Nova Scotia College of Art and Design], but my dad said that he would pay if I went to McGill [to take medicine]. He said he wouldn't pay if I went to NSCAD, so that helped shape my decision to go to McGill.

Employment Opportunities

The labour market that participants encountered upon entering the workforce strongly affected the employment opportunities that were available to them. Their labour force participation was further impacted by the educational credentials they held and their family obligations.

Labour market

The strength of the labour market determined the quantity and quality of job opportunities available for participants. Those living in the robust economic conditions of Calgary, for example, had both more employment opportunities in terms of numbers and more choice in terms of variety than their counterparts in the Maritimes. In weaker job markets, participants vied to get the attentions of employers, competing for fewer job openings against more experienced workers with the same/similar qualifications.

Kate, who was living in Halifax, had a master's degree in counselling and related work experience. Despite her qualifications, she hadn't been able to land a job as a therapist after six months of trying:

I have a strong skill set. I have amazing reference letters and I've been getting good job interviews. But nothing is coming. They're telling me that I don't have enough experience at the post-graduate level. I think that people look at me and see that I look young, that's part of it. But it's my lack of experience is what I've been hearing.

Kate's story stands in sharp contrast to participants, like Jason, who lived in Calgary and seemed to have easier access to better-paying jobs that required fewer credentials and less work experience. Jason had recently started a job as a manager in Calgary with no experience or formal training. According to him, he was "unbelievably unqualified to be doing what I'm doing."

Several participants noted how entering the labour market during a recession impacted on their career trajectories. Gazal, who had graduated with a master in public administration degree, spoke about how the recession impelled her to enrol in a social work program:

I felt like I was competing against people that had experience and the same level education as well as a better idea of what they wanted to do. I felt like the niche in the labour market for that specific area was already so small. So the recession in 2008–09 was kind of my demise. I think it also shifted my interest. Looking back, I think if I had gotten exactly what I was looking for or I had graduated in 2003 or 4, I would have stayed in that field and moved from there.

Even in a buoyant economy, not everyone had an easy time finding satisfying and sustainable work. Nadia relocated to Calgary, expecting she'd cash in on the boom times. She discovered something different:

You can't expect to get into a job that is specifically what you want right away. You have to start with something. I think it's a big misconception that it's so

CHAPTER FOUR **51**

easy to get a job, easy to make lots of money. It's not. Living expenses are a lot higher, even though you may be making more money. So it's not easy.

Educational credentials

Most participants in this study, like young people their age nationally, had obtained a university degree or college diploma, or were in the process of doing so. The type of credential participants held varied from those that were occupationally-directed such as engineering technology, accounting, or auto body repair to general arts and science degrees and diplomas. A minority of participants had either dropped out of post-secondary education or had never attended.

Some participants who didn't have post-secondary credentials felt that it limited their options; others did not. Oliver expressed his frustration with being locked out of jobs for which he thought he had the skills:

What's holding me back from doing what I want to do would be to have more education. Had I decided right after graduation that what I wanted to do was be a computer network technician, then I would have gone and gotten all the certificates. The only thing that's stopping me now is having a piece of paper that says I can do what I know I can do.

Not surprisingly, those who didn't feel disadvantaged by not having post-secondary education were in careers that didn't require formal credentials. Ben, an entrepreneur, was a good example:

I'm glad I never went to post-secondary education. A lot of people that I have met spent more time doing that. While they were in school, I was working full time. At the end, a lot of people that I see, I'm more ahead than they are.

For some participants, deciding to attend post-secondary education immediately after high school seemed to depend on their level of confidence in their academic abilities. Typical of this sentiment was Donalee who deferred entering university because of her lacklustre marks. She chose instead to work, then ease into the post-secondary world by way of a few courses before getting the confidence to enrol as a full-time student. Now armed with a bachelor's degree, she was poised to continue:

Now I want to go into social work; I'm going to apply for grad school next year. But, at the time, I didn't do very well in high school. I had mediocre to low grades and I didn't enjoy school. Part of not wanting to go to university right away is that I didn't think I could do it.

Overall, those participants with more specialized credentials, such as professional degrees, technical college diplomas, and trades certificates, had an easier time finding satisfying, full-time work that related to their training.

By contrast, many general arts and science graduates, even some from Calgary, found it difficult to find employment or were in jobs where they were underemployed—either because they didn't know what kind of jobs they were seeking, or employers didn't perceive them as being qualified. Alan, a political science major, offered his take on how employers viewed a general undergraduate degree:

I think there is some kind of impression that it's just a stepping stone; it's grade 13. I've heard it referred to as that. After I finished my BA, I was looking for a job for the summer and I can remember employers saying, "Oh, that's just a BA." It was just basically the same as a high school diploma.

Family responsibilities

Many participants were married or in common-law partnerships by their mid-to-late twenties. A sizeable minority had children. Some had taken on parenting responsibilities in their late teens or early twenties, while most had waited until they were in their mid-twenties or older. A few were caring for parents, grandparents, or siblings.

For the female participants in the study, in particular, the demands of parenthood or caring for family members significantly influenced what employment or educational opportunities they pursued. Female participants who were parents were more likely to have reported leaving the workforce completely or cutting their work back to part time to accommodate the demands of family.

Stacey, a stay-at-home mom, described what her return-to-work priorities were going to be:

When they start school, I might work part time, wherever. I just don't want to be working six o'clock at night when they're home. My husband is on a weird shift, so the less babysitters I've got to pay for, the better.

On the other side, some male participants said they felt they needed to take the best-paying job possible, not necessarily the preferred one, in order to support their family.

Impact on strategy utilization

Participants like Kristen, the chemical engineer from Calgary, smoothly navigated with their sought-after credentials into a labour market clambering for their skill sets. Others with equally "marketable" qualifications lived in areas of the country where constricted employment opportunities made it difficult to navigate and commit to their chosen fields.

Anna, who lived in Halifax, aspired to be an environmental scientist. She described her on-again, off-again career track:

I got two degrees and then I kept getting contract work with the Department of Natural Resources. It would be six months here, one year there, sometimes

lot of new arts and science graduates:

I started working part time at the group home and I was working at the mall too. Part way through the year, I got really sick of going between the two employers. I got double-booked at places, despite my best efforts, and it got really stressful. I looked into other jobs and discovered you might apply fifty places and get no calls unless it's retail, or something that isn't very good money, not enjoyable, and the hours aren't very good.

it was only for a couple of weeks. I started to work at the movie theatre, just to tie me over between contracts. Then, my programs were cut quite a bit and they didn't have money for me.

At the same time, the manager of the movie theatre left and I got offered the position. It was just the right time because I knew I wasn't getting anything from Natural Resources for awhile. So, I became salary at the movie theatre, which had nothing to do with what I want to do. But I kept looking for environmental work.

Many participants with general undergraduate degrees were living in the topsy-turvy world of underemployment, settling for whatever work was on offer. Being stuck in unrelated or low-skilled work didn't give them the opportunity to build up the solid work experience they needed to competitively navigate into more rewarding careers.

Celeste, with a bachelor's degree in psychology, was typical of a

Limited job opportunities made it more likely that participants would employ a settling strategy. A few expressed having "given up" trying to find a satisfying career. More common was the sentiment of "settling for now," with the idea that they would eventually find something more attractive.

Mike, a qualified golf course manager who couldn't secure a stable income in the golf industry, settled for work as a fisherman's helper in order to support his family. The

biggest barrier to finding viable work, according to Mike, was "just living on Prince Edward Island because it's just so short-based [seasonal]. It's hard to find a good career. Right here doesn't leave me very many options."

Some participants who lacked educational qualifications drifted from one low-skill/low-wage job to another. It was like that for Adrian who had been adrift since leaving school. For the past three years, he had worked at a car dealership doing small repairs and cleaning. Because he had no formal credentials and limited marketable skills, he had few prospects for improving his situation. He described the result of drifting this way:

Most of them were just dead-end jobs. I probably shouldn't have even bothered with them. It wasn't what I wanted to be doing. I haven't done anything really meaningful career-wise. In the time I've had, I could have done a lot more than I did. But, I just go day to day.

Family responsibilities seemed to constrain the process of navigating for some participants, while being facilitative for others. Many said that, once they were in a serious relationship, they needed to factor their partner's needs into their plans. It might, for example, be necessary to pass up a good job opportunity or attendance at a university of their choice if their partner was unwilling/unable to relocate.

Others had to care for ailing family members. Carly was accepted into a nursing program, but she opted not to go:

I declined the offer because my grandmother was sick. Then my grandfather got sick and I chose to stay home to be with them while they were still here. When they both passed away, I didn't have an opportunity to do the course. So, I just gave up the dream.

A number of women related that having children had motivated them to return to school to improve their employment qualifications. They wanted a career that offered pride and financial stability for their families. Val described how having children propelled her to begin navigating:

If I didn't have my children, I do not believe that I would be a resident care worker. I didn't mind working at housecleaning or whatever. It made the difference because I thought, "I am out slaving and this just isn't going to pay off. My kids deserve more." So I think that was basically the driving force.

CHAPTER FOUR 55

degree and trying, unsuccessfully, to find work in the field that appealed to her.

Recently she had become interested in working with animals and wanted to explore that option to see if it might be more meaningful. She said that it wasn't as easy since getting married: "I have to be more calculated about exploring and go about it more intentionally. The question is, given my responsibilities, how can I satisfy my curiosity?"

Family responsibilities also influenced participants' decisions to settle for the work situations they were in. Rebecca explained the connection between her father's death and her decision to settle for a job she didn't particularly like:

When my father really became sick, I returned home. I would never consider that an obstacle. It was a huge learning experience for me and something I'll never regret. I decided to stay home after that to be close to my mom. That's why I'm still here: to help her and support each other. Because of that, I took a job which sort of relies on previous skills. I'd already decided that I didn't want to be in the field that I am currently in, but I fell back on that because it was a good job. I know it's sort of settling for the time being, but for the right reasons.

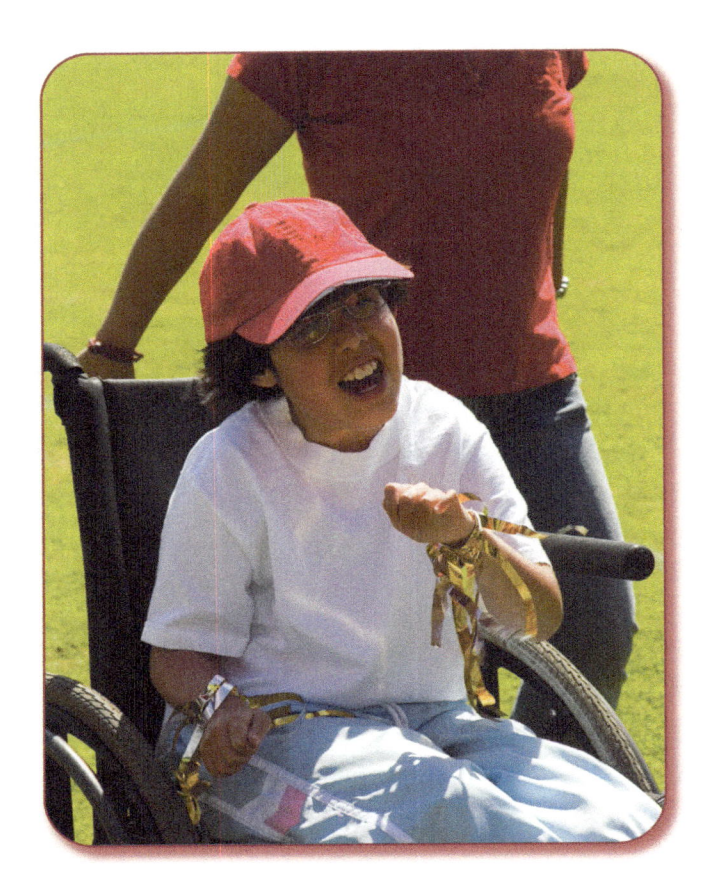

Some participants felt that, once they took on family responsibilities, the time for exploring their options was beginning to run out. Maggie had spent much of the preceding decade in exploration, by taking a social work

Chapter Five
Shifting Places

I think drifting and exploring for awhile and then navigating is cool. Kind of like getting thrown off a ship. You drift for awhile and then think this is getting a little boring so maybe I'll swim this way for a little bit. Then you're like, it's definitely this way and you swim to shore.
― Colin, a 26-year-old from Halifax

The previous three chapters described the process by which participants found a place and the influencing factors that impacted on their career journeys. For the sake of clarity, the strategies and factors were discussed primarily in isolation of one another. By doing so, there is a danger of losing the most important finding of the study: the strategies and influences interacted with and informed one another in complex and unpredictable ways.

In this chapter, a case study is presented that illustrates how one participant moved back and forth between strategies and was influenced by different factors to varying degrees at different points along her journey.

Drifting

Megan had "no dreams, no goals, and no plans" when she graduated from high school. Her school years were difficult: she was bullied emotionally and physically and she did poorly academically. She had no friends and was "socially handicapped" when she graduated. Megan's experience in school left her with little confidence: she didn't believe she was capable of doing anything beyond working on a road crew or an assembly line.

One of the few positive things Megan had in her life during high school was the emotional support of her mother and step-father. As she put it, they "built me up after I would come home everyday in a puddle" and constantly told her not to "let 'them' win."

Megan hadn't planned on pursuing post-secondary education because of her poor high school marks and lack of confidence. However, her mother was adamant that she acquire skills that would make her self-sufficient.

Megan had no idea what interested her, so her mother decided that a computer technician program would be a fit with her personality. Her mother took matters into her own hands, phoning and going to the local college to get her registered. There was a waiting list, but her mother persuaded the college to accept her and paid the tuition.

Megan wasn't particularly interested in the program, nor did she think she was capable of doing it. She agreed, however, to give it a try because she believed that there were no other options open to her.

Upon graduation, I didn't know what I was going to do. I thought about going back to high school for a year, but my mother said "you've got to do something." My mother managed to get me into a program at the community college. I at least could feed myself and that was the plan. I actually would have some sort of a job.

Most of her classmates were older than Megan and they offered her support and encouragement. Much to her surprise, she excelled in her studies and her self-confidence grew. She began to consider applying for jobs in her field. Graduates in previous years had had a hard time finding good paying jobs, but Megan's class was fortunate to be graduating when a new call centre was recruiting in their community. She was offered a job, which she accepted, believing it was the best opportunity available to her.

Settling

Megan didn't like the work at the call centre, but she saw it as a career because it was "the place to work" in her community.

I thought that I was lucky to get into the community college and now I've got a career. I figured I was done. At the time, it was a horrible job. I hated it. I was upset, became stressed out. But, as a kid 18 years old, clearing $1,500 every two weeks, that was a lot of money. I thought I was on top of the world.

The call centre job proved to be instrumental in Megan's personal growth. She said that "it provided a protected environment where I could recover from high school." She developed a group of supportive friends who "coaxed me out of my shell." They even introduced her to the man who would later become her husband.

Megan had a talent for dealing with angry customers who regularly took out their frustration on whoever was on the other end of the phone. She attributed her ability to deal with the abuse to the "tough skin" she had developed from years of being bullied in school. Her supervisors praised her skills and hard work, and her confidence grew from the positive feedback:

I had no confidence before I worked at the call centre. I was shy, I was very reserved. When I walked away, "nothing can faze me, I'm bulletproof."

Four years on the job and Megan had become frustrated. Despite being the most qualified candidate for a promotion, she was passed over for the job. Her supervisor told her it was because of her age:

I was overlooked because of my age constantly. Everybody said that I should be promoted. I was top notch and I really do believe I was excelling at what I was doing. But a 40-year-old didn't want to listen to a 20-year-old.

I could never advance, even though my record and my skills showed that I should be. Everybody treated me as a supervisor, but they were never going to promote me. They'd always give it to somebody older, more mature.

Another promotion opportunity came and went and Megan was overlooked again. A co-worker told her, "You're too good for this place" and suggested she consider going to university. Megan thought it was a joke: how could she get into university with her mediocre high school marks? Her co-workers informed her she could apply as a mature student.

Megan discovered that she could try out some university courses in spite of her previous academic performance. She took an English course and found it easier than she had expected.

Encouraged, she enrolled in a bachelor of science program because she thought her interests might lay in one of the health care professions. Megan continued to work at the call centre full time to support herself while going to school.

Exploring

Once in university, Megan volunteered at the hospital to get a better sense of which health care professions she might be most interested in. She considered massage therapy and physiotherapy; her mother vetoed her choices because she associated them with working in a massage parlor. In retrospect, Megan thought that these occupations may have been a good fit but, at the time, she wasn't prepared to resist her mother's sentiments.

In the summer of her second year, Megan had the good fortune of being accepted into a government-sponsored program designed to expose students to a range of health care professions. It was here that she became interested in becoming a physician.

Megan's first two years at university were challenging as she acclimatized to academic life, at the same time maintaining a full-time job. On top of that, she struggled with health issues.

Several times Megan considered quitting and settling for working at the call centre. A professor explained that the first two years were a "weeding out" process and that her final years would be easier. This encouragement, coupled with her husband's support, kept her going.

I really wanted to give up. I didn't want to do it anymore and he told me that I just couldn't give up. He helped me see that I could do more than I give myself credit for.

At the end of third year, Megan planned to continue working at the call centre and volunteer at the hospital. On a whim, she applied for and got a summer job as an environmental field worker through a government internship program. It was an area she knew little about, but she quickly discovered that she both enjoyed and was good at it. Megan was offered a full-time contract position after she graduated.

Do I Settle or Navigate?

After working in government for two years, Megan felt that she was at a crossroads. Her job had become routine and stale. For the work she wanted to do, she needed to have graduate qualifications. With a PhD, there would be "limitless opportunities" and she "could write her own ticket" in environmental science. Unfortunately, her funding for graduate school didn't materialize.

Megan's interest in medicine also resurfaced after a family member was treated for a serious illness. She had been told by several medical schools that her work experience would make her a strong candidate, but she would need to improve her grade point average in order to be competitive. By Megan's estimation, that would take two years of coursework.

Megan was crushed that the selection criteria was weighted so heavily on academic marks and that her work history and research experience didn't count for more. By maintaining a full-time job throughout university, she had not only hurt her chances of getting into medical school,

CHAPTER FIVE 59

but also of being "at the front of the line" in terms of graduate school. Had she known, Megan said that she would have focused more on school and less on working.

At the time of the follow-up interview, Megan had turned 30. Her outlook was undergoing another shift. She and her husband were hoping to start a family in the next few years. Still interested in medical or graduate school, Megan was seeing her options "starting to slip away." It was a case of "panic time, do it now or never." Her husband was supportive of whatever she chose to do, but Megan wanted to be a "devoted mother" who stayed at home while her children were pre-schoolers.

She was feeling torn between the options in front of her. In her view, staying in her present job was "selling out" because it was not something she found challenging or rewarding. On the other hand, she was hesitant to quit because the job offered good benefits, including maternity leave. She was also concerned that going to graduate or medical school would be a financial strain on her family, at least in the short term.

When asked how she would decide either to settle in her job or navigate towards medicine or a PhD, Megan said that she had confidence that "hints" would appear and that it would become clear about what to do.

Megan's Points of Transition

Megan's story illustrates some of the key points of transition in which participants moved from one strategy to another.

Megan's launchpad was less than auspicious. A traumatic high school experience, with attendant poor grades, had left her feeling that her lot in life was taking whatever low-skilled jobs came to hand. Through her mother's insistence and interventions, she drifted into a college program that she knew nothing about, wasn't interested in, and didn't think she was capable of handling.

College was a turning point for Megan. She was successful in her studies for the first time. She made friends and her confidence grew. She had the good fortune to graduate at a time when there was a hiring drive in her community and she managed to land a decent-paying job. Had she not gone to college and had the call centre not been hiring, she would likely have ended up drifting from one minimum wage job to another.

Once Megan got the job, she moved from drifting to settling. She didn't like the work at the call centre, but she settled because she considered it was the best opportunity available.

By the time her co-workers suggested she contemplate university, much had changed for Megan. Her skills and confidence had continued to grow, as had her disillusionment with being overlooked for promotion. Armed with the encouragement and support of family and workplace friends, Megan was primed to move from settling to exploring. It is interesting to note that Megan said she might still be at the call centre had she received the promotion.

Megan's exploring activities included testing university academics before enrolling full time; volunteering at the hospital to learn more about health professions; participating in a health-care career exposure program, and being introduced to environmental science through a summer job. One missed opportunity lay with her mother's misperception about massage therapy and physiotherapy: by Megan's own assessment, these might have been fitting options. During this phase, Megan might well have moved from exploring back to settling had her husband and professor not encouraged her to stick with her studies.

At the time of the follow-up interview, Megan's perspective had taken another turn. Having turned 30, she was on the threshold of moving from exploring to navigating or settling. She knew that career advancement, whether in environmental science or medicine, required advanced training. She also knew she needed academic upgrading to be a competitive candidate for either program.

There was a sense that exploration time was running out and she needed to make a decision. For Megan, there were conflicted emotions: "I would love to do medicine, but it involves such a big chunk of time." Had Megan not needed to commit two years to improving her marks to compete for admission into medical school, she may well have chosen to navigate towards medicine. She was in the unfortunate position of knowing what she wanted to do, but feeling that she may have to settle with what she had in order to be able to move into a "family phase."

Finding Their Place: Shifting Strategies and Influences

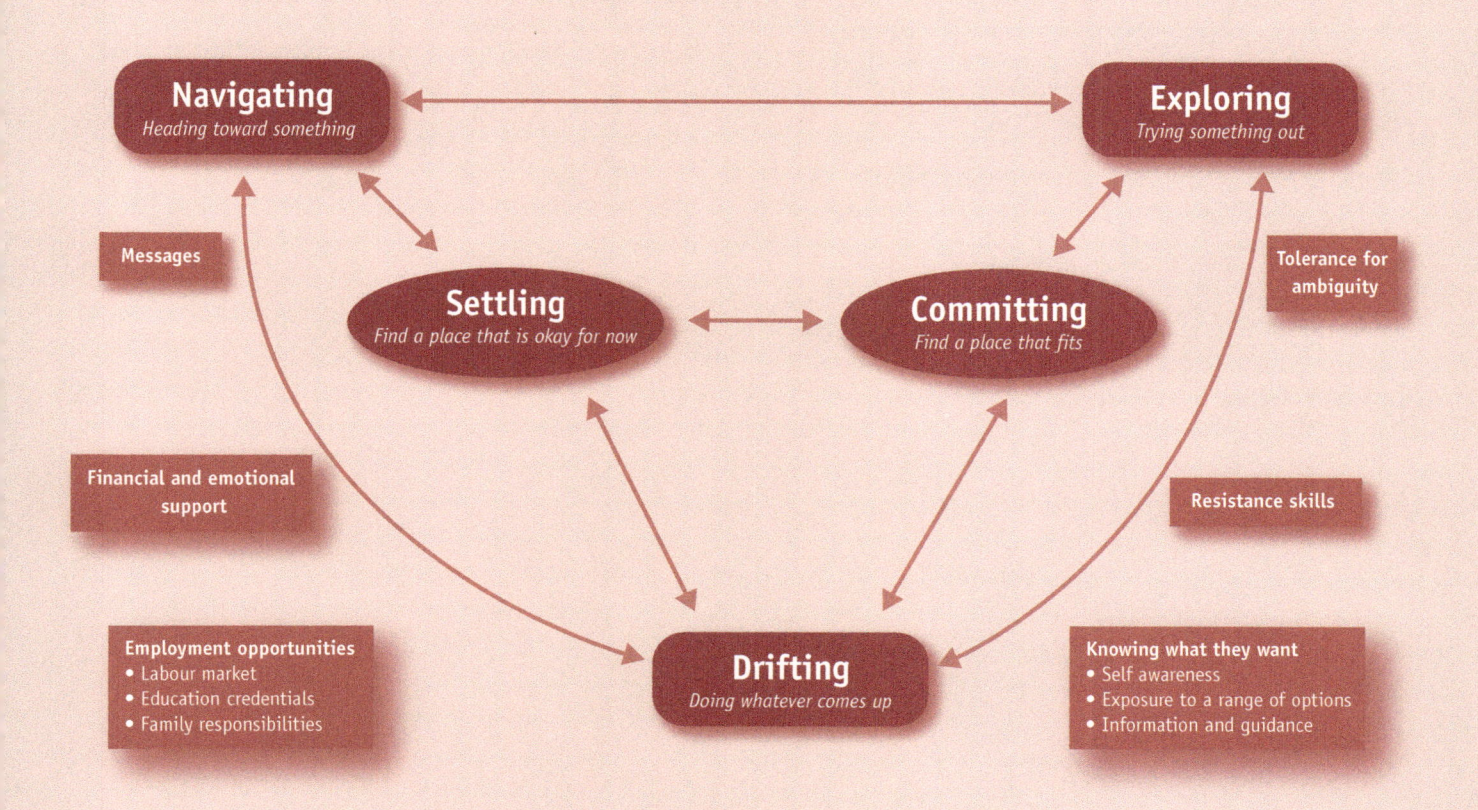

Navigating — Heading toward something

Exploring — Trying something out

Settling — Find a place that is okay for now

Committing — Find a place that fits

Drifting — Doing whatever comes up

- Messages
- Financial and emotional support
- Employment opportunities
  - Labour market
  - Education credentials
  - Family responsibilities
- Tolerance for ambiguity
- Resistance skills
- Knowing what they want
  - Self awareness
  - Exposure to a range of options
  - Information and guidance

Megan's career journey is typical of many young people starting out. As they encounter new experiences, opportunities, and life circumstances, their self and career awareness evolves. At different times, they will use different strategies in their ongoing pursuit of finding a satisfying place.

The study indicates that the following points of transition were present in the career journeys of participants.

If they were **Navigating**, they sometimes changed to:

Committing as they learned more about the realities of what they were navigating toward and realized it was a good fit.

Settling, *Drifting*, or *Exploring* as they learned more about the realities of what they were navigating toward and realized it didn't fit with their goals.

Settling if they were cajoled by others to continue in a field that didn't interest them or if they had a low tolerance for ambiguity and weren't comfortable reopening the question of what they were going to do.

Drifting, *Exploring*, or *Settling* if their chosen career path wasn't accessible (e.g. debt, low marks, family responsibilities, critical messages, low self-confidence, or not being able to find a job in their field).

If they were **Exploring**, they sometimes changed to:

Navigating or *Committing* if they found a career path that was or they believed would be satisfying.

Drifting or *Navigating* if they became frustrated with not finding a suitable path.

Settling if they weren't able to determine what they wanted to do; if they took on family responsibilities that required them to stay in a job they didn't enjoy, or if they didn't have the internal or external resources to pursue their preferred career option.

If they were **Drifting**, they sometimes changed to:

Navigating if they discovered education programs or work opportunities that interested them.

Committing if they liked the field in which they were working.

Exploring if they became more proactive about determining the type of work they wanted to do.

Settling if they weren't able to determine what they wanted to do or if they took on family responsibilities that required them to stay in jobs they didn't enjoy.

If they were **Settling**, they sometimes changed to:

Exploring or *Drifting* if they lost their jobs or began to find their jobs intolerable.

Navigating or *Exploring* if they were encouraged to examine their interests and options.

Committing if something shifted in their job and it became more satisfying.

If they were **Committing**, they sometimes changed to:

Exploring, *Drifting*, *Navigating*, or *Settling* if they lost their jobs or started to find their work less satisfying.

Navigating if they found new fields of work they preferred.

Settling if they had to take better paying, less satisfying work because of family responsibilities.

Chapter Six

Career Crafting Techniques

If I could do it all over again, I would definitely have looked for guidance when I graduated from university. This would have given me some semblance of where I was going rather than being like a fish out of water trying to fight for myself.
~ David, 30-year-old from Halifax

Rethinking the Ways We Work With Young Adults

It is clear that young people's career journeys take many unexpected twists and turns. A brief conversation with the right person or an unexpected job offer might turn out to be pivotal to figuring out a career direction. A poor labour market or rejected application to graduate school might put a halt to career plans that have been carefully constructed up to that point.

Nonetheless, the pervasiveness of the Career Myth means that many young people, and those who support them, continue to believe that it is possible to follow a predetermined straight-line career path in the immediate years after high school graduation.[1]

The reality of change and unpredictability is not new to the career development field. "Change is constant" is a phrase that has been bandied about so much that it has become a truism. Knowing that change is constant is not particularly useful for young people when they are confronted with expectations that they should have long-term, linear career pathways and feel the urgent need to make a decision.

Young people need direction on how to work with uncertainty in a way that goes beyond platitudes. They need tools not only to take informed action, but also to help them weather the uncertainty and changes of heart that will likely characterize their career journey. Too often, we career professionals acknowledge that young people's career journeys will be circuitous and unpredictable, but then turn around and use the same methods that have been used for decades.

Despite the obvious limitations of a career counselling approach that attempts to match people with careers, the method continues to be widely used. One need only look at the websites of most high schools and post-secondary institutions to see that young people are typically told that good career decision making occurs as a result of matching traits (such as values, interests, skills, and personality styles) with the factors required to successfully perform a particular occupation.

Given the tenacity of the Career Myth, it's not surprising that this attitude dominates the public's thinking about the school-to-work transition. If young people and their parents believe that career pathways are supposed to be linear and unchanging, it follows that they would presume that it's possible to be matched with a suitable career.

Moreover, career counselling approaches that emphasize certainty and promise neat answers are attractive to people who are rattled by the uncertainties and complexities of life. Little wonder then that young people want (and expect) counsellors to give them the answers. Career professionals themselves perpetuate the belief that young people can be matched with certainty to occupations when their primary intervention is to administer a battery of career inventories.[2]

This is not to say that we need to jettison the interest inventories, values exercises, and skills and aptitude assessments that are in most career professionals' tool boxes. But we do need to reconsider how we think and talk about uncertainty and change with the young adults we work with. The same could be said for clients of all ages, but it's particularly important for those of us who work with young adults because unpredictability and change is a defining feature of the early stages of their career journey.

The challenge for career professionals is to find a viable alternative to the Career Myth. What do we offer young people, if not the mythic idea of security and certainty? We need to help young people accept that there will be a certain amount of disorder in their career journeys, at the same time encouraging them to look for the underlying patterns and themes that are expressed through their interests, values, and preferences.

Recent decades have seen strides in the development of career counselling approaches that embrace unpredictability and change rather than trying to keep them in check through attempts to develop long-term career plans. Major contributions that support this new line of chaos-friendly approaches include:

- H.B. Gelatt who gave us the term "positive uncertainty" and who suggests that people should head off in the direction of their career goals while staying open to the possibility that they will change their minds on the basis of new information or as circumstances change.[3]

- John Krumboltz who maintains that career development, at core, is a learning process and that emphasizing the next step as opposed to the final destination will do much to alleviate the anxiety many people experience.[4] Along with two colleagues, Krumboltz also highlights the role of happenstance in people's careers and recommends that people create their own luck by strategically doing things that increase the chances that positive unexpected events will occur.[5]

- Danielle Riverin-Simard who offers the idea that vocational identity provides hidden order to people's seemingly disordered career journeys in that a person's identity may change over time, but not generally in dramatic ways.[6]

- Robert Pryor and Jim Bright whose Chaos Theory of Careers suggests that people's careers constitute a complex system in which many factors impact on one another in intricate ways which, in turn, lead to unpredictable outcomes.[7] They emphasize the impact of the "butterfly effect" that is characteristic of complex systems which means that a small incident (such as a chance encounter) can produce a large variation in the outcome (such as entering a career field not previously considered).[8]

- Katharine Brooks who further operationalizes the use of chaos and complexity theory in career counselling with the development of her "Wise Wandering" coaching system.[9] She advocates for "experimental wandering" and "intention setting" which increases the chances that positive unforeseen opportunities will be noticed.

- Herminia Ibarra who argues that the conventional wisdom that we must first know what we want to do before we can act has it backward.[10] Knowing, she says, is the result of doing and experimenting. Ibarra contends that, because so many new ideas and bits of information surface once people get moving, that spending too much time upfront figuring out "the plan" wastes energy. She advises people in the midst of a career decision to get out of their heads and begin to take action (test-and-learn rather than plan-and-implement).

Collectively, these chaos-friendly approaches normalize the convolutions that characterize young people's career journeys. They make it clear that long-term plans don't make a lot of sense when there are so many wild cards that can profoundly impact on what happens. At the same time, they emphasize the need for young people to take action even as they wade into the sea of uncertainty.

The strength of more traditional approaches is the emphasis they place on identifying people's vocational personality which can provide a compass to guide young adults' decision making and thereby lessen the chances they run aground.

Marrying the strengths of both approaches allows counsellors to help young people embrace the vicissitudes of their career journeys while still providing a means by which they can recognize what's discernible in their lives that can guide them as they proceed.

Career Crafting Techniques

The results of this study highlight the importance of normalizing unpredictability and change in the school-to-work transition and providing young people with tools to work more effectively with this reality.

In the pages that follow, a series of strategies called Career Crafting Techniques is presented. These techniques counsel young people to recognize the need to take action in the face of uncertainty rather than spend too much time and energy trying to "figure things out." In taking action, young people learn about themselves and make it more likely that positive unplanned events will occur that lead them to satisfying work.

From the work of Gray Poehnell and Norm Amundson, the term "crafting" was intentionally chosen as an alternative to the more traditional words, planning, management, or decision making.[11] Crafting removes the inference that one can predict and control the future and emphasizes the uniqueness of individuals' career journeys, as well as the proactive notions of practicing, doing over, mastering, and creating as they go along. The idea of crafting is in line with the reality that most young people construct their careers from the opportunities that are available to them rather than choosing a career pathway.[12]

Woven through the Career Crafting Techniques are the recurring themes of "Doing" and "Reflecting" on what's next. All too often, young people do one without the other. Those who do without reflecting rush around doing education and career-related things in a frantic haphazard way. By doing so, they often fail to take full advantage of the opportunity for learning about themselves and the possibilities that are available.

Those who reflect without doing try to think their way to satisfying career decisions and never venture out to test the suitability of their choices. For many, it becomes a case of, "the more I think about it, the more confused and frustrated I get." Then, when their choices don't work, they are left feeling even more baffled and anxious.

The Career Crafting Techniques offer a way for service providers to integrate chaos-friendly career counselling approaches into their existing practice. They allow the career professional to retain many of the tools and processes they are accustomed to using while strengthening their utility. By shifting the focus from determining a goal and mapping a plan, these techniques allow the

Career Crafting Techniques

DOING
- Know that it will be a journey
- Actively look for what sparks your interest
- Develop a "shopping list" to guide your journey
- Experiment with intent
- Create your own "lucky breaks"
- Take another step
- Plan with a pencil
- Do what you love somewhere in your life

REFLECTING

counsellor to continually focus and re-focus the young person's attention to what they have learned so far and what they need to do next.

Forefront in the thinking of each technique is the emphasis on doing first, reflecting second; being strategic about what they are doing; keeping change and unpredictability clearly in the picture, and continuing to move forward in the absence of having made a firm decision.

Know That It Will Be a Journey

Young people, and those who support them, need to understand the nature of the journey on which they are embarking. Given the prevalence of the Career Myth, it's not surprising that many young people are shocked to find that their career journey shares little resemblance to their expectations. Adding insult to injury, they get blamed (and blame themselves) when their career journeys don't match the dictates of the Career Myth.

As Stephanie observed, knowing that it is a journey doesn't mean it is easy to accept:

I see my career as a destination, not a journey. Because of the way I was brought up, finishing my bachelor's was a destination. I know it is not a reality but, in my mind, I think it is. So it is a paradox of what the reality is and what my expectations are.

Your career journey will likely take many twists and turns

Some young people do make the transition from school to work in a linear fashion. But this is an anomaly due more to good fortune than skillful planning.[13]

For others, things go according to plan after high school when they enrol in college or university—up until the time they graduate. That's simply a continuation of the roadmap that has been set out. Where things start to get really challenging is what happens after leaving post-secondary when their degree or diploma doesn't land them satisfying work. They are sent back to the drawing board, having to rethink their options and figure out what they will do next.

Figuring out what you want to do takes time

Young people are often under a lot of pressure to have an answer to the ubiquitous question, "What are you going to do?" Some are expected to have the answer when they graduate from high school. Others are given some leeway while they are in college or university, but the pressure mounts as they near graduation. There is a sense that they are magically supposed to have figured it out.

In reality, it takes time to figure out what type of work might be personally satisfying. Generally, young people need to learn more about themselves and the options available to them. That means they need to get out into the larger world and try out different things. This, in turn, takes time and patience both on the part of the young person and people around them.

Therese Schwenkler, a 30-year-old blogger and life coach, reflected back on her years of struggling to figure out what she wanted to do:

I wondered about this crap for well over five years before anything began to make sense. It's maddening. You want to wake up tomorrow and jump out of bed shouting, "Aha! Finally I know what I was put on this earth to do." But, let's get real. It takes time to figure things out—usually years, not days. What I need to do, despite it being the most difficult thing to do, is not to plan, but to accept that "I don't know."[14]

It's common for young people who have gone through the turmoil of milling and churning to reflect, with regret, that they "wished they knew then what they know now." They feel that they could have been spared the pain, expense, and wasted time of false starts if they had known out of high school what they wanted to do.

But, it's not possible for most 18-year-olds to make well-informed, long-term career decisions because their identities are evolving and they have a limited view of the opportunities that are available to them. Even if they are able to make career decisions that seemingly fit, factors beyond their control, like a downturn in the economy or a family crisis, can stymie their efforts and change their plans.

Your career journey will be unique to you

Rarely do people successfully execute career journeys entirely on their own. The experiences of others are insightful. Sound information and advice is helpful. Encouragement and support is invaluable. But each young adult faces a set of conditions that is unique to their circumstances. Just because a particular route worked for a friend or sibling doesn't mean it will work for them.

Nor should a young person compare their career journey's progression unfavourably to the "progress" of others. What may appear to be someone who has it all together and is making all the right moves might be someone who has seized upon a closest-at-hand career plan to allay their anxiety. Or it might be someone whose plan works fine up to a point—then gets derailed by any number of unexpected events.

In the final analysis, each young person must move along their own pathway, in ways and within a timeframe that fits their situation.

The journey is often uncomfortable

If we accept that there is a great deal of uncertainty associated with young people's career journeys, it follows that it will be an uncomfortable process. Anxiety is a pervasive state that many young people feel as they grapple with the messages that are inherent in the Career Myth.

They feel discomfort when they are asked what they want to do and they have no answer. They worry whether or not they've made the right choice, if they will fail in their chosen pursuit, if their loved ones will disapprove of their choice. They are disappointed and blame themselves when their efforts don't measure up. They become disillusioned and resentful when reality sinks in and they discover that doing what they were "supposed" to do hasn't resulted in finding satisfying work.

Ethan described what it felt like "being off the path":

It's terrifying not knowing where I'm going to end up, not knowing what I really want to do. You look at other people and they're working and becoming successful. That's the terrifying part: getting left behind.

Strategy: As career advising professionals, a key issue is to continually work at normalizing what young people are experiencing. This is critical if they are going to have a fighting chance of fending off the unrealistic expectations of the Career Myth. Application deadlines, pressures from parents, mis-information, and comparisons to friends can conspire to short-circuit your efforts.

More than likely you will need to reiterate the messages we've presented above. You will want to:

- point out that it may take some time for them to figure out what is right for them.
- help them resist the urgent "need to decide right away" when they grab onto a hurried choice or map out a detailed, long-term plan before they are ready.
- let them know that, despite the best planning, unplanned events may occur and that they should expect to encounter the unexpected somewhere along the way.
- let them know that it won't always be evident where their efforts are leading. There may be times they feel they're spinning their wheels, going sideways, or even sliding backwards.
- reassure them that things tend to sort themselves out as they become clearer about what's important to them and what opportunities are available to them.

Strategy: An evocative way to normalize what young people are experiencing is to show them the Career Myth graphic on page 95. First, fold or cover the bottom half of the graphic and show them the top half. Then, ask them to determine to what extent they have felt the expectation that their career journey should follow this linear progression.

CHAPTER SIX 67

Next reveal the bottom half of the graphic that illustrates the circuitous way that most young people's journeys actually unfold. Ask them to reflect on the degree to which this represents their experience. If their journey has been meandering, rather than linear, enquire about the impact the expectations of the Career Myth has had on their thinking and feelings.

Young adults who have been shown this graphic seem to visibly relax when they realize that their experience is normal rather than disordered. Being able to visually see the disconnect between the expectation and their experiences helps them to understand why they have had so much angst about their education and career paths.

Strategy: Another approach that helps normalize young people's experience is to show them the graphic, Finding Satisfying Work: Which Strategies Are You Using? on page 96, which depicts the five strategies we have discussed in previous chapters. This technique can be particularly useful after a young person has shared with you the career journey they have taken thus far. You would then describe the strategies and enquire how, if at all, they have used any of them in their bid to figure out what they want to do.

It's important to emphasize that the strategies are offered as a map of what young people are doing, rather than an attempt to pigeonhole them. We often find that they are using two strategies simultaneously. For example, Carlos chose to "navigate" toward a career as a researcher by doing a doctorate in chemistry, at the same time he was exploring the possibility of becoming a veterinarian by volunteering at the SPCA. Working on his PhD freed him from the pressure of having to answer the question about what he was going to do while he remained uncommitted to that choice and continued to explore another option.

You would then discuss the factors that are impacting on the strategies they've used. This can be enlightening to the young person. For example, Jeff the musician in Chapter Four, registered three times for a college program to pacify his mother, but backed out at the last minute each time.

When Jeff was introduced to the strategies and influencing factors, he indicated that his primary strategy had been to drift from one thing to another. He knew that being a professional musician was what he wanted to do, but the message he received was this wasn't a valid choice.

Enrolling in a trades program was Jeff's attempt to follow a route that those around him approved of, but then he would get cold feet and withdraw. Identifying the dynamics in play helped Jeff realize that he wanted to pursue a career in music, but he needed to find some way of supporting himself and managing the negative messages he was receiving.

Strategy: It can be encouraging for young adults to hear stories of the convolutions and uncertainties in other people's career journeys—particularly of those a few years older who have gone through similar experiences and are now more established on their career paths. You can share the stories (without identifying details) of other young people you have worked with and encourage them to open up their own conversations with older young adults.

Even conversations with parents about their career journey experiences can be eye-opening. Robin recounted how encouraging it was to hear his parents speak about things not being as effortless for them as they appeared:

It helped a lot to know that they weren't always so sure in their paths or that it took them a while to get there. My dad applied to med school two or three times. My mom changed because of my dad. So I was like, "I'm going to be okay."

Simply knowing that what they are experiencing is normal can be a big help. In the course of vetting the research results with young people, most said that it was reassuring to know that their experience was similar to others their age. The fact that this had been documented through a research project seemed to lend a lot of credibility to the message.

Strategy: So many of the young people interviewed for this study mentioned how having, or not having, emotional support impacted on their confidence and motivation to proceed on their career journeys. David spoke about how important his support system was after he'd been "beaten down" and "kicked to the curb" by four less than stellar job experiences in a period of five years:

Without a support system you just crumble. If you have a support system, it just makes life so much easier. When you're struggling you can go to someone and say, "Hey I'm struggling with this" and they let you know they've been through it. Or they've gone past it and can tell you it will get better.

Because so much of the doing and reflecting that young people undertake is a solitary activity, many feel alone in their endeavours. What they need, between sessions with their career advisor, are regular doses of encouragement and a supportive sounding board to keep up their momentum. They need to know that their career journey isn't a "do-it-yourself" project. And they need to be encouraged to initiate and maintain contact with people who are their allies: those who will listen to and acknowledge their concerns without judgment and who can offer inspiration, information, and advice because they've "been there."

Actively Look for What Sparks Your Interest

A major dilemma for many young people is that they are trying to make career choices without being clear at all what interests them. This was certainly the case for many of the young people interviewed for this study. It was particularly evident in their reminiscences about leaving high school, but it also continued as they moved in and out of post-secondary studies—and into the workforce.

Administration of an interest inventory may uncover some of their interests, but often they haven't had enough experiences to know whether or not something does (or could) hold their interest. The fact is, they can't know in advance what is going to really interest them and they can't know in advance what type of exposure may kindle an unbeknownst interest.

One of the most pervasive obstacles career advisors face in having young people identify their interests is getting them unplugged from the technologies that are so prevalent in their lives and plugged into expanding their horizons. Another issue is convincing high school/post-secondary students and young workers that they need to carve out some space in their busy schedules that is free from diversions and makes room for exploration and discovery.

"Doing" takes an abundance of free time. Young people need to expose themselves to many new things even though they might not know if they'll find them interesting.

CHAPTER SIX 69

It also takes undistracted time where the young person can come to appreciate, without urgency, whether or not their interests warrant exploring further.

Doing, without urgency: there's another rub. Many young people feel the pinch to bypass what might be considered frivolous adolescent dreaming in favour of coming to a firm "adult" decision and making a plan. Whether it is pressure from family or anxiety from within, many young adults can't relax enough to engage in what could be a lengthy process of self-discovery.

Strategy: Working with young people who don't have an inkling of their interests may feel like something of a scavenger hunt as you try to help them latch onto something that captures their attention or piques their curiosity. The germs of an abiding interest may come from anywhere, no matter how seemingly insignificant.

A good place to start is with activities they have chosen to do in their own time and in their own ways: memories of hobbies and pastimes from younger years, current pursuits, people they admire, some part of their school experience. When people do things they want to do, purely for pleasure and satisfaction and freed from what others may say or think, they are expressing natural interests that distinguish their personality from others.

The following line of questioning may inspire a young person to look more closely at the activities they've been doing to get clues about their interests: What did you enjoy doing when you were 10? What do you choose to do when it's completely your own free time? What are you doing when you feel most "yourself?" What things have you wanted to do, but haven't had the chance? What is it about these activities you find so appealing? What else might you do that would allow you to pursue these interests?

Some young people haven't had much in the way of non-school pursuits, or are blasé in their recollections of them. The career advisor's role is to encourage young people to move beyond their familiar confines in the hopes that a spark will ignite. By beginning to look and do, they may accidentally "bump" into some interesting person or activity that they don't usually come across in their everyday lives.

That can include taking a single course; attending campus open houses or industry expos; joining school or community clubs, teams, groups, or causes; talking to people doing work that intrigues them; connecting with others through special interest on-line forums, or volunteering with any number of community organizations. The goal is to get young people "out there," to take notice of what's going on and who's doing what, and to discover what, in all of that, they naturally gravitate towards.

There are no easy solutions to the challenge of young people being distracted, overscheduled, and overwhelmed by the expectation to make a quick decision. It is important, however, to let them know that slowing down and spending time upfront trying things out and getting a sense of what interests them is time well spent.

Develop a "Shopping List" to Guide Your Journey

It wasn't uncommon for participants in this study to graduate from high school and enter post-secondary education with vague notions about what interested them, what they might be good at, or what might be important to them in terms of a career. Many were overwhelmed by information and the number of choices available to them and anxious about making the right choice.

Many bounced from one program to another in an attempt to gain clarity. Some graduated from programs no wiser about what they wanted to do than when they first entered.

Being able to generate, explore, and evaluate possible career options is a crapshoot when young people haven't developed a set of criteria to guide their decision making. A lot of time and money can be wasted as they wander in the wilderness. A lot of frustration, disappointment, and regret can build over "mistakes" made and missed opportunities.

The term, "Shopping List," is used as a shorthand way of describing the patterns and themes (interests, abilities, values, temperaments, environments, etc.) that develop over time and which reflect a young adult's vocational identity.[15]

The beauty of the Shopping List is that it takes the pressure off young people to make far-reaching decisions and encourages them to have an ongoing dialogue about what they really want their life to be like. The more the conversation about their future revolves around identifying those elements the young person prefers—as well as those they want to minimize or avoid—the less likely they are to fixate on having to make a hastily-conceived, ill-informed, long-term career decision.

The Shopping List isn't a roadmap to a particular destination, but rather a frame of reference that can be brought into play at every step along the career journey. By assembling, in one place, the key elements that the young person would like to have in their work life, they are more apt to be able to identify (or begin imagining) education/work options that might align with what they are seeking. They also have a more articulate "vocabulary" when engaging in career conversations with others which, in turn, increases the chances that others can constructively contribute suggestions that relate to their criteria.

This expanding inventory of career possibilities can be captured in what has been referred to as an "Explore List," a record of jobs, occupations, and non-work roles that share some of the characteristics that the young person has identified.[16] By developing an Explore List, the young person can focus their research and experimentation activities on those options that show promise, but which still require further investigation to determine their viability.

As exploration turns to evaluation, the Shopping List becomes a touchstone which young people can use to sift through and assess the information, advice, and experiences they've encountered. Most importantly, it gives them insight into why particular options on their Explore List might or might not fit.

As a result, the Shopping List lets young adults become "choosers" rather than "pickers."[17] Instead of picking from what's readily available, they can choose based on the set of criteria they have personally developed. It offers young people greater confidence that the choices they decide to navigate towards, if not certain matches, are reasonably aligned with what they know about themselves and what they've learned about their options.

The Shopping List isn't a set-in-stone epithet. Certain elements, such as core interests, may change little, if at all, over time. Other elements, however, will as young people are exposed to new information and experiences, as their identities evolve, and as their circumstances change.

What was unimportant at one stage of their life may become critical a few years later (or vice-versa). Significant events both positive and negative—like marriage, parenthood, divorce, job dissatisfaction, financial pressures, or newly discovered opportunities—may alter the look of the list considerably. Young adults will need to continually review and refine their Shopping List and generate new options for their Explore List to accommodate these new realities.

The process of developing the Shopping List and Explore List is very similar to the traditional approaches career service professionals use to help young people choose a career. There is the same need to increase their self-awareness, to translate their interests and abilities into suitable education and work options, and to increase their knowledge of what's out there. The difference is that you aren't asking them to make a decision, but rather to identify options that make sense to research and try out. That is far less anxiety-provoking.

The case example on pages 73 and 74 illustrates how a career counsellor used the three strategies discussed below to help a client develop a Shopping List and Explore List to guide her career decision making. Blank copies of the two lists are provided on pages 97 and 98 if you want to use this technique in your practice.

Strategy: An effective way of helping young people develop a Shopping List is a process modeled on Norm Amundson's pattern identification exercise in which clients' life experiences are used to reveal themes that are relevant to their career journey.[18]

The first step is to ask the young adult about some activity from leisure, education, or work which has been particularly enjoyable. Then ask them to think about what they found so appealing about that experience. Their response forms the start of the Shopping List.

Then ask them to identify other gratifying activities, past and present, from different aspects of their life. Taking each activity in turn, have them mind map what, in particular, was satisfying about that activity. These statements are added to the Shopping List. Items that recur amongst the activities are noted with a checkmark as many times as they appear.

As well as identifying what's enjoyable, it's important that you encourage young people to reflect on what activities they strongly dislike and would want to avoid in a work environment. Frequently, the opposite of what they dislike is something that they want. These revelations can be added to the Shopping List.

Given its simplicity, this activity is a surprisingly potent and time-effective method for ascertaining themes and patterns that have threaded throughout a young person's life. The exercise works equally well with individuals or groups; it can be used by itself or in conjunction with the use of traditional career counselling tools such as card sorts and standardized assessment tools. The first time that the exercise is completed it is helpful to demonstrate how the young person should proceed.

Strategy: After the Shopping List has been sufficiently developed to show patterns and themes, it can be beneficial to have a young person draft what Mark Franklin refers to as a "career statement."[19] In creating a Career Statement, Franklin suggests that young people highlight those elements they want to have, those activities they want to do, and those talents they want to use. The Career Statement, written in point or paragraph form, becomes a summary of the most important things a young person is looking for.

Strategy: You can help young people generate options for their Explore List by probing for ideas they already have, by brainstorming through a mind map exercise, or by referring to any career assessments they've done that suggest possible occupations or leisure pursuits.

Once the Explore List has been created, have them do some preliminary research on-line, in print, or through information interviews with people in the field that address the following questions: What are the main duties? What skills are needed? What training/qualifications are needed? Where is the training offered? Length? Cost? What are the job prospects like? What does it pay?

On the basis of their research, certain options may be eliminated as being unappealing or unviable. New options may be discovered and added to the Explore List. With the information they have gathered, have them consider to what degree each option meets what they are looking for. The objective is to narrow the list down to a manageable number of options that warrant more in-depth experimentation.

All too often young people in this study related stories of career assessments being used in isolation. A list of possible occupations was generated, but little assistance was given to help them understand what the results meant. Some reported that it was a frustrating experience because the career assessment matched them with obscure or seemingly inappropriate occupations like dolphin trainer, florist, or funeral director.

Others said that the career assessments identified occupations they were already considering, but did nothing to help them work through the confusion they were feeling about which one to pursue. Most didn't receive any help in understanding why particular occupations were rated higher than others. Rather than broadening their thinking about what they could do, the career assessments restricted the options for some participants. Emile, reflecting on taking an interest inventory, said:

It said that I liked working with people and that I should be a firefighter. That would have been great, but it's kind of stereotypical. Working with people: I could have been a team manager, I could have been a social worker, I could have been so many different things. But it went "ding, firefighter."

The comments of those participants who found assessment tools helpful are instructive for career professionals. They said that, when an advisor used the assessment results as part of a broader counselling process, they were able to better understand how the resulting list of occupations related to their self-profile. They also found it helpful when the counsellor brainstormed with them a range of education and career possibilities that went beyond those generated by the test. And finally, participants appreciated getting guidance as they conducted their research and help in sorting out which options made the most sense for them.

Case Example:
Shopping List and Explore List

During the intake assessment, it was revealed that 23-year-old Jen had come to career counselling because she was dissatisfied with her job as an administrative assistant. She was considering a number of career options including social work, nursing, teaching, and police work. Because she hadn't determined any criteria for making a career decision, she was feeling overwhelmed by the options and unsure how to proceed.

Through mind mapping, Jen was asked to determine what she found so appealing about the options she was considering. Helping and making a difference were themes that surfaced, which were recorded as the start of her Shopping List.

When asked to identify activities in various aspects of her life that she found particularly satisfying, Jen came up with this list: camp counsellor, camp program director, Canada World Youth participant, hiking, and being an elected student union representative. She was also asked to identify two past activities that she strongly disliked and she identified a university accounting course and a retail job in an outdoor equipment store as being particularly unsatisfying.

For homework, Jen was asked to mind map what she found appealing about each of the positive experiences she had identified and what she didn't like about the negative experiences. During the second session, Jen shared the results of her mind mapping exercise (a sample mind map is shown below).

The positive and negative items Jen had identified from her mind maps were added to her Shopping List. Items that were similar or repeated from one mind map to another were clustered together and their frequency of appearance was indicated with a checkmark.

Over the next few sessions, Jen completed a values card sort, a skills card sort, the Strong Interest Inventory, and the Myers-Briggs Type Indicator. The results of these assessments confirmed many of the criteria that were already present on Jen's Shopping List which helped ground the results in her own experience. As before, new information coming from the assessment tools was added to the Shopping List and recurring items were checked to indicate how frequently they appeared.

Jen's completed Shopping List is shown on page 74. You can see the clusters of similar statements and how frequently each item emerged during the assessment process. Jen then reviewed the statements and highlighted those that best described what she was looking for. With the counsellor's assistance, she created a Career Statement that summarized the elements of a work role that were most important to her. Jen's Career Statement is shown at the end of her Shopping List.

The Shopping List provided Jen with insight into why her job as an administrative assistant wasn't satisfying. While the job met her criteria for interacting with people and having regular working hours, it didn't give her a sense of making a difference in people's lives.

The counsellor next took Jen through another mind mapping exercise to develop an Explore List of possible occupations that she might investigate further. They reviewed the occupations she had initially identified. In reflecting on the results of the Strong Interest Inventory, Jen was interested to note that she shared similar patterns of interests to people who worked in those occupations. Looking over her Career Statement, Jen wondered now if they might be too structured for her liking, but she decided to leave them on her Explore List for the time being.

Jen was then asked whether she was curious about any of the other occupations the career assessments had identified and she added a number of those to her Explore List. With the counsellor's help, she then brainstormed other options which she also added to her list. Jen's completed Explore List, comprised of options from her own original ideas, career assessments, and brainstorming with the counsellor, is shown on page 74.

Jen then undertook some preliminary print and on-line research on her Explore List options and conducted information interviews with people working in the field. Her counsellor advised her that it was unlikely she would find

CHAPTER SIX 73

Career Statement (diagram spokes):
- Social Worker
- Nurse
- Teacher
- Police Officer
- Psychologist
- Physiotherapist
- Community Organization Director
- Lawyer
- Activist
- Mediator

any one particular career option that would fulfill all her key items and that she would need to seek other avenues in her life to satisfy those requirements that weren't met through work.

Based on her research, Jen eliminated police officer, nurse, psychologist, physiotherapist, and teacher from her Explore List as they didn't fit the prioritized criteria she had set out in her Shopping List. The options remaining warranted more in-depth experimentation to determine their viability and compatibility.

Jen reported that her anxiety was greatly reduced by having developed the Shopping List and Career Statement that gave her touchstones for assessing whether the options on her Explore List were a good fit or not.

Jen's Shopping List

<u>Make a difference</u> ✓✓ help society ✓✓ help people ✓✓✓ improve kids' and staff camp experience ✓✓

Work with people ✓✓✓✓ public contact/<u>lots of interaction with people</u>

Work as part of a team ✓✓ work closely with other people ✓✓✓ teamwork

Take a leadership role ✓✓ initiate change ✓✓ make decisions/ systemic change

Opportunity to create new ways of doing things ✓✓ innovate/<u>coming up with creative solutions to problems</u> ✓✓✓✓ opportunity to be creative

<u>Variety of tasks</u> ✓✓✓✓

Facilitate groups ✓✓✓ teach/train ✓✓ mentor ✓✓

Unhappy when constrained to strict schedule or mundane tasks ✓✓ dislike performing routine tasks

Dislike being micro-managed ✓✓ need independence to complete tasks/little supervision ✓✓

<u>Flexibility but need to have some structure to get things done</u>

Dislike strict regimentation and hierarchy

Appreciated for the work I'm doing

Excitement/taking risks

Speaking to groups

<u>Travel</u>

Outdoor activities / be physically active

<u>Regular work hours</u>

<u>Time to spend with friends and family</u>

Career Statement: I most want to make a difference in people's lives by helping individuals or communities find innovative solutions to their problems. I want to have lots of interaction with people. The work environment that would suit me best is one that has flexibility and variety, but I do need some structure in order to get things done. I want my work to give me the time and resources to spend time with family and friends, do outdoor activities, and travel.

Experiment with Intent

Chapter Two described three strategies that young people use to find satisfying work: navigating, exploring, and drifting. Those who were exploring overtly experimented with different education and work options, without being sure of the outcome. Those who were drifting took whatever happened to come along but, they too, were conducting experiments of a sort. If they were lucky, they stumbled into an occupation that fit; if not, they stayed with what they had or tried something else.

For those who were navigating, there was an assumption that they were clear about their desired outcome and the pathway to get there. In reality, many of them were experimenting as well. They didn't know much about the path they had chosen, whether or not they would like it, be any good at it, or it would work out for them.

Hence, the recommendation to conduct experiments is really asking young people to do what most are already doing. The advantage of advising a young person to conduct experiments rather than make a firm decision is that they don't feel as beholden to it. Instead of having to say to the people around them, "I've changed my mind," they can simply say, "I explored the option and it didn't fit." It is much easier for a young adult to say the latter, change course, and continue experimenting as circumstances warrant.

As was said, young people are already conducting experiments to figure out what they want or to test drive an interest. Unfortunately, what's going on a lot of the time when they're job surfing or switching education programs is aimless, expensive, and time-consuming experimenting. Winston, who spent his time milling through jobs, succinctly put it this way: "If I like it, I'll stick with it. If I don't, I'll have to look somewhere else. That's all I can do. One of these days, I'll find the right thing."

Even when they enter the job market with credentials that seem tailor-made for them, young people continue to experiment as they begin building their careers. So much of the success of their career journey depends on landing a job in their career field, finding a workplace where the "culture" fits their personality, finding the right niche within their field, not becoming burned-out, bored, or disillusioned with the realities of the work, and so many other factors. In this regard, it's fair to say that few of us ever make a final career decision and that many of us continue to experiment with new occupations, new organizations, or new roles within our existing organizations.

Strategy: Considering how much experimenting goes on—and for how long—the suggestion here is that young people become more intentional about the experimentation they do.

There certainly is considerable overlap in the types of activities that young people participate in when they are exploring for interests and when they are experimenting with intent. Exploring for interests is a more free-wheeling activity where a young person is encouraged to sample many different experiences, not necessarily knowing what might capture their attention and not necessarily being concerned that the experiences have any future career applicability. Some activities will reveal a genuine attraction, while others will be discarded as being uninteresting, of lukewarm interest, or a passing fancy.

Ideally, exploring for interests results in the start of a Shopping List of preferred criteria and an initial Explore List which is refined on the basis of research. For those education or work options that continue to show promise after preliminary research, young people need to be able to immerse themselves more fully in situations that allow them to experiment on a practical level. It's only by

Career service practitioners are also pivotal in helping young people process the learning that emerges from their experimentation through the following line of reflective questioning. What more did you learn about yourself? What more did you learn about the education/work options you were considering? Are there more criteria you could add to your Shopping List? On the basis of what you've learned so far, how do the options on your Explore List fit with what's on your Shopping List? Did you discover new, perhaps better, possibilities in the process of experimenting that should be added to your Explore List? What more can you do to investigate these new options?

The new learning that emerges from each experiment supplements and brings further focus to the evolving Shopping and Explore Lists. It also provides guidance in generating ideas for their next steps. Over time, the young person becomes clearer about a direction. Experimentation becomes more trial and less error until a voice inside them says, "I'm on the right track."

Strategy: It's not uncommon for young people to be challenged by their early work experiences. Many find the workplace a bewildering and alien environment. Some have little idea what to expect and others have expectations that aren't always realistic.

getting some level of "insider" knowledge that a young person can judiciously assess whether or not an option is something that could sustain their interest, that they are able to do, and that they want to navigate toward.

Career professionals can be assistive to young people by helping them strategically devise a series of practical trial and error experiments. Who could they talk to or connect with on-line who could offer expert information or advice about a field of interest? What courses could they test out that best fit their interests or develop their expertise? For liberal arts and science students, in particular, what courses offer some type of experiential learning?

Are there opportunities to arrange a workplace tour or job shadow with a company that does work that interests them? Is it possible to do an internship or co-op placement or get a summer, part-time, or volunteer job in a work environment of interest?

What community groups or organizations are they drawn to? What volunteer activities within these organizations would give them practical experience that best relates to their interests and the skills they would like to develop?

76   CAREER CRAFTING THE DECADE AFTER HIGH SCHOOL: PROFESSIONAL'S GUIDE

If they are fortunate, new workers have the benefit of orientation and job shadowing to learn the basics of the job and the rules of the workplace. Some are left on their own to pick it up as they go along.

What's harder to figure out and cope with is the workplace culture with its seemingly arbitrary unwritten rules, elements that often have nothing to do with the work itself. With little employment experience and unaccustomed to working environments, it can be especially mystifying (and unsettling) for young people to comprehend such intangible factors as bully bosses, sabotaging co-workers, inter-departmental turf wars, and personality conflicts.

Many feel powerless (or don't know how) to handle inappropriate behaviours or challenge injustices. Frequently their response is to simply shut up or leave, fearing that speaking up will jeopardize their position or future prospects.

Early negative work experiences can impact the way young adults view their job or their employer. They can sometimes be pivotal in convincing a young person that a career field isn't right for them. In cases of clashes with a boss, they can even signal the end of a career before it's had a chance to really get started. Like Taylor in Chapter Four who aspired to become an art curator. Her early experience with an abusive boss left her utterly demoralized, out of a job, and terrified that her reputation had been ruined in the local art world.

While a young person is still experimenting and available to you, it's important not merely to debrief the work content of their experiences, but the work culture aspects as well. You need to be able to help the young person separate the valuable work experiences, accomplishments, and personal growth derived from the experiment from the intolerable environment in which they worked. They need to understand that they shouldn't rashly eliminate an option on the basis of a single experience.

On the other hand, young people also need to understand that some dynamics are common to many work sites and that they will need to learn strategies to deal with them in the future. Strategies such as minimizing the time spent with a problem person; keeping communication logical and fact-based; avoiding topics that get them into trouble, and understanding and accepting the person "as they are," may be useful tools that the young person can take with them into their next experiments.

Strategy: Of particular concern these days is the increasing numbers of young adults who find themselves in survival jobs to pay the bills and entry-level jobs that don't relate to their training or don't offer avenues for advancement.

It's easy for young people to slip into a dissatisfied, but complacent attitude about their work situations. It's also easy for the years to slip by unnoticed, only for them to wake up and realize that their credentials are now stale-dated and thousands more young people with fresher credentials have flowed onto the market to compete with them.

Underemployed young adults still haven't landed in a career place that fits and they still need to experiment in order to find that place. What most of them are seeking is a better job. But better jobs don't just come along. Before that happens, a person has to figure out how they can get better for that next better job.

The BA graduate who has spent the past five years working at a call centre is going to face quite a challenge convincing employers that their experience is germane to work as a research assistant. Having done research for university term papers likely isn't going to cut it.

Volunteering to produce a credible research report for a social cause, offering to analyze the data collection questionnaires at work, and conducting survey interviews as a casual job will add more weight to this arts graduate's resume.

Young workers caught in dead-end and incompatible jobs need to be encouraged to reinvigorate their experimentation activities—and to commit to sticking with it.

Create Your Own "Lucky Breaks"

Lucky breaks appeared in the stories told by many of the participants in this study. A classmate's job tip. Accidentally landing on a valuable career website. A fortuitous missed application deadline. A replacement instructor's inspiration. Kayla talked about how she got a lucky break that took her from working at a call centre after graduating with a master's degree to teaching at a university:

I'm a go-getter. If I want something, I'm going to fight for it. I ended up going back to the university I graduated from and spoke to the Dean and said, "I need a job. If you don't give me a job, I'm going to have to move to Calgary and we do not want that." And he said, "You're right, we don't. Give me a few days." Then I got a job as a professor. Pretty much they made this position for me where I travelled to Aboriginal communities and taught people that had just come out of high school.

Lucky breaks are frequently associated with getting a job or getting a better job. But they are equally important when it comes to strengthening one's application for competitive education, youth exchange, or career exposure programs, and for securing coveted internships or volunteer experience opportunities. Lucky breaks also appear when experts are willing to offer young people the benefits of their experience in the form of insider information, advice, and contacts.

Often, lucky breaks really are a matter of being in the right place at the right time. That initial lucky break opens up an opportunity. However, what happens after is not luck. It's the combination of right attitude and right action.

People who consider themselves lucky "expect" good things to happen.[20] They assume that the more opportunities they encounter and the more receptive they are to those opportunities, the "luckier" they can expect to be. They are actively on the look-out for opportunities and they intentionally create situations to increase the possibility that opportunity, in the guise of a chance event, comes into their lives.

Lucky people are open to meeting new people, participating in new activities, and paying attention to their surroundings. Strictly from a numbers perspective, this proactive mindset is likely to produce more lucky breaks than a passive approach that stands back and hopes something great will happen.

For starters, they need to have some idea what "better" means to them. By developing or revising their Shopping List they may become more focused when it comes to determining what it is they are seeking. They then need to intentionally choose trial sites to explore, ones that will place them in environments and among people where it is more likely they will uncover the kinds of information, contacts, and possibilities they need to set them on a new course.

As a career service professional, you can help young underemployed workers see their way out of their disheartening situations. How can they get value add-on experiences in their current job? How can they target their networking efforts to increase the chances of having a lucky break encounter? What volunteer activities or sideline work opportunities can they incorporate into their schedules that offer skill development or exposure to a sector they are interested in?

Dissatisfied young workers may feel stuck in a rut and use their job commitments as an excuse for not having time to undertake experiments. Career practitioners can acknowledge that time constrictions make it challenging, at the same time encouraging them to find the time to schedule in experiments that matter. By bringing meaning to their every day, they might start to feel that there is hope and that their efforts will lead to something better over time.

Traditional goal setting involves deciding what you want to do and then setting SMART goals that are specific, measurable, achievable, realistic, and time-bound. SMART planning makes sense when the steps to reach a goal are straightforward, such as credentials to become a physiotherapist or mechanic.

Intention setting, on the other hand, doesn't involve developing a specific game plan for getting there. This approach is particularly useful when it's not obvious how a young person will get where they want to go, for example, landing a job as a journalist in a tight job market or working as an outdoor adventure therapist.

The young person who has set their intentions knows what they are looking for and is more likely to "see" a related event or person than someone who hasn't. This relates to selective perception where we begin to notice things that were always there, but we just weren't looking for them. For example, the young adult who has a Career Statement that relates to being a coach is far more likely to spy a bulletin board notice recruiting volunteer soccer coaches than someone who isn't fully aware they would like to coach.

If a young adult's lucky break involves people—getting advice, learning about an opportunity, or being mentored—then they can only get lucky if they meet the right person.

Still, 1,000 friends on Facebook and a congested calendar won't bring luck through the door if a person doesn't know what they are looking for, doesn't recognize opportunity when it presents itself, and doesn't know what to do with it when it comes knocking.

Strategy: There is no "to do" list that will directly manufacture luck. However, there are things young people can do to increase the chances of them catching a lucky break. Simply being out there doing lots of things and meeting new people will increase the likelihood that a positive unplanned event will take place.

It is even more likely to occur if the young person has identified what they would like to happen through what Katharine Brooks refers to as "intention setting." What they set their intentions around could be a short-term horizon like, "I want to get a summer job working with kids" or longer term such as, "I want to work overseas as an engineer." Developing a Shopping List that is crystallized into a Career Statement is a particularly effective way of setting intentions.

CHAPTER SIX **79**

But they can't run into the right person without meeting a lot of people.

Career advising professionals should encourage young people to talk to everyone they know or meet about what they would like to do in the future. The more people they meet, the greater their odds of getting lucky. Ethan talked about taking to heart the advice he had received after participating in a career launch program for post-secondary graduates:

I've been networking like crazy, just trying to meet as many people as possible. I want to be so well networked that I won't have to be filling out cover letters and resumes. I think that, most of the time, how people get jobs is just through people they know.

A place to start is to get a young person's current circle of contacts working for them. The graphic below shows how networks spiral out from family and friends to school, work, community, and beyond to strangers one meets at a social function or waiting in line at the bank.

Each person in a young person's network has their own network of contacts. If a young person can articulate what they are looking for, the ripple effect of expanding networks exponentially increases their chance of catching a lucky break. David spoke about the power of networks when you know what you are looking for:

If you have an idea of what you want, it's really easy to get guidance. You can ask around until someone knows someone who knows someone who knows something about something. If you walk in and say you don't know what you want to do, nobody can help you because they don't know what to do. If you make it a challenge for them, they're not going to want to do it.

Knowing what you want and meeting people are critical to opening up opportunities. But it takes a certain amount of confidence and finesse to set the stage that turns an opportunity into a lucky break. It requires that the young adult steps forward and shows genuine interest in the person that represents that opportunity. It requires that they share information about themselves and how their interests and aspirations align with what the person can offer. In short, it means establishing a sincere relationship so that people respect the effort that has been made and are more likely to offer their time, knowledge, and advice.

Who is in your network?

- You
- Family
- Personal & family friends
- Friends' friends
- Friends' family
- Instructors & classmates
- Neighbours
- Coaches & teammates
- Church & club members
- Parents' employers & coworkers
- Your employers & coworkers
- People where you volunteer
- Internet web sites
- Professional organizations
- Casual acquaintances
- People with whom you do business
- People doing work that looks interesting
- You get the picture

This material is available courtesy of the Nova Scotia Community College.

[Staircase diagram with steps labeled alternately "Take another step" and "Learn from it"]

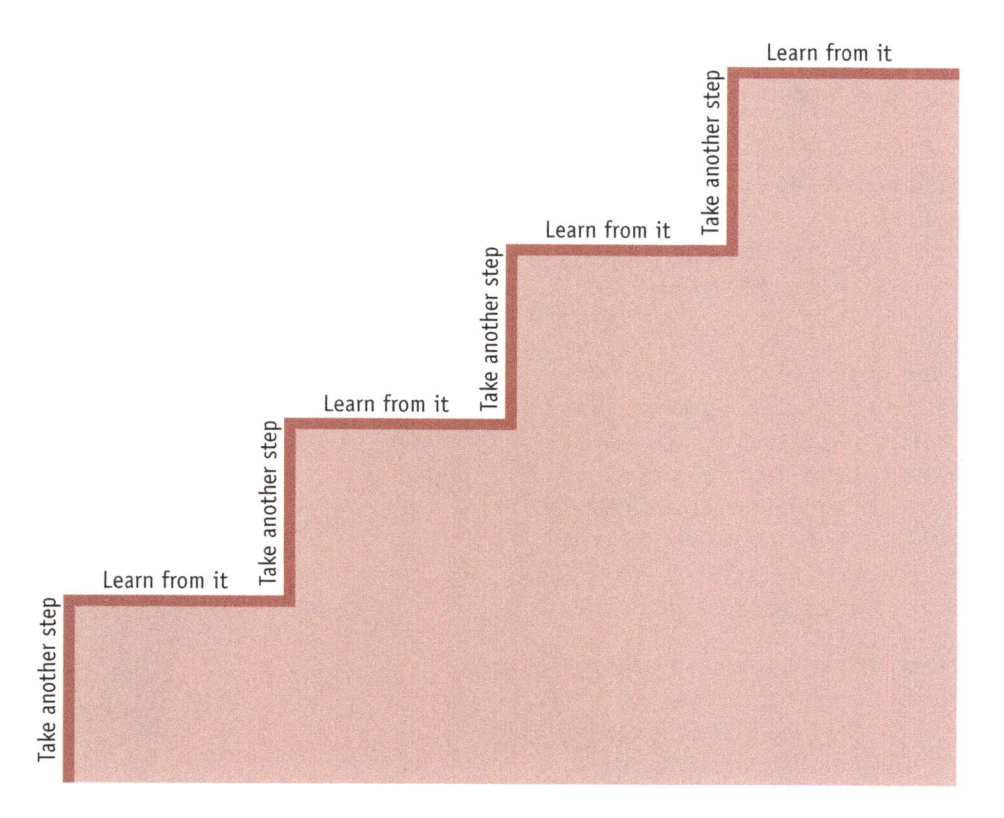

Take Another Step

Most participants in this study ended up following career pathways that they hadn't planned to pursue when they left high school. Their plans evolved and transformed as they gained more experience and their circumstances changed. Given that most young adults' career journeys are unknowable from the outset, it would seem wise for them to focus on incremental steps and decisions, rather than on long-term career planning.[21]

As long as young people are dwelling on missteps from the past or obsessing about the future, they are distracted from focusing on the here and now. By concentrating on one step only—the immediate next step—young people are able to break decision-making into do-able bite-size pieces, rather than becoming overwhelmed with making the right, best, or lasting Big Decision.

So, the key is to start doing. And keep doing. That first step could be trying out a single university course, taking up a new hobby, joining a club, travelling, volunteering, or getting a survival job. By taking the first step, young people start learning new things about themselves, the work that others do, and the work that might be satisfying to them.

They can't know the consequences of taking that first step before they do it, but the new learning that comes from it will feed the next step. If an area of interest is revealed, what next step might confirm the depth of that interest? What next step might demonstrate whether one has the ability? If it reveals no interest, what next step might uncover a new avenue to explore?

Strategy: From your reflective conversations with a young person, you will be able to ascertain how well they know themselves, how much they know about the realities of the options they are considering, and how committed they are to those options. Have they developed a Shopping List? Does their Shopping List give them a good sense of what they are seeking? Have they created an Explore List? Is that list congruent with their Shopping List?

On that basis, you can help a young person identify what the logical next step would be so that they aren't randomly pursuing a bunch of activities that don't add up to much in the end. Do they need more or better information about a work or education option? Where would they get that? Do they need more or better experiments to clarify their interests? Where would they get that? Do they need to be encouraged to look at other options? What other options might be appropriate and what should they do first to explore that?

Wherever they are in the process, the young person needs to be encouraged to take that next step and to reflect upon what they learn. Apply the new learning and take another step. Learn from that and take another step. And so on.

If each new step, taken in turn, incorporates the learning from the previous one, it is more likely that the steps will build upon each other. Gradually, as the young person becomes clearer and more confident which options have the greatest validity, a "plan" will begin to unfold and take form.

Strategy: A pressing issue for many young people whose steps, to date, have involved post-secondary education is the size of their accumulating debt. Looming repayment schedules force many to take the first, or best paying, job available rather than continuing to experiment with options for better fit. It compels some to forego training that might improve their marketability and pushes others to stay in school to forestall having to start making loan payments.

As part of taking another step, young people should be advised to keep an eye on the growing size of their student debt and not to put it on the back burner to be dealt with another day. Living frugally is a whole other book, so we won't go there. Suffice it to say that young people should be encouraged to live like students when they are one and only slightly better for the first few years after they enter the job market.

It can take years to pay off student loans. The sooner they are able to battle their debt down, the sooner they will be free to contemplate other adult milestones like marriage, children, home ownership, and savings. They will also have more flexibility to consider getting more training or taking "better" jobs that may be lower paying.

Another aspect of debt management relates to return-on-investment. For young people who aren't ready to enter post-secondary or are using college/university as a means of finding out what they want, there may be poor returns on their investment. As Armand said, "You spend $40,000 on university. I didn't get my $40,000 worth of university."

Taking another step for some young people may be assessing the value of their being in post-secondary education *at this time*. Perhaps a time-out travelling, working, or getting involved in some near-and-dear special interest project would be a more effective, less expensive way of gaining self and career clarification.

For debt-straddled diploma and degree holders who are considering advanced studies, another step might be to carefully investigate what advantages, financial and otherwise, accrue to graduates who have that credential. Do the returns justify the added schooling costs? Would there be benefits to postponing further studies if they could enter the career field in some capacity and get a clearer focus on what specific training would best move them towards their goal?

Plan With a Pencil

Young people in the study frequently navigated towards occupations they knew little about and, somewhere along the line, many realized it wasn't what they wanted to do. Some changed course, while others doggedly continued on because of the message that they should just finish it off.

Other participants, no matter how focused and hard working they were, had their career journeys derailed by forces outside their control: not getting accepted into the education program they chose; not having the funds to see their training through; not being able to find a job in their field; having a traumatic experience with a boss; being laid off from a job they loved; having to care for ailing family members, or dealing with their own health issues.

Facing up to the reality that a dream goal is, at best, on hold and perhaps permanently shelved can be devastating. For some young people, not being able to let go of a dashed dream keeps them in limbo and immobilizes them from carrying on with future planning.

The fact that goals often change and plans never work as neatly as they appear on paper is no reason to abandon planning altogether.[22] Goals provide direction and the motivation to put in effort. Direction and effort result in more opportunities. Opportunities lead to better information gathering. Better information leads to more directed actions. And so the momentum builds.

What's important, however, is that young people not become rigidly locked into one pre-determined goal, rejecting the possibility that new information or alternatives could come to light or factors outside their control could influence the outcome.

It was H.B. Gelatt who first asserted that career goals were best approached with "positive uncertainty." Positive uncertainty requires that young people remain, paradoxically, both focused and flexible. By knowing what they want, but not being too sure, they can treat their goals as hypotheses—educated guesses about what they'll do and what will occur. This allows young people to be motivated, but not limited, by the goals they have set and the plans they have made.

Gelatt suggests that young people should develop "flexpertise" when making decisions about the future when they don't know for sure what that future will be.[23] By that, he means they need to be able to work with ambiguity and remain open-minded to exploring new territory and learning unexpected things. Most of all, they need to be able to change their mind, adjust their expectations, and alter their course of action if circumstances show grounds for it.

Strategy: As a metaphor, "pencil planning" is a powerful way to position all the career planning activities that a young person will undertake. Pronouncing a career goal at age 18 doesn't mean a young person will be accepted into the training. Entering university doesn't mean they will exit a graduate of that same program. Earning a post-secondary credential doesn't mean they will be consigned for life to that particular career field.

The concept of pencil planning works for young people whose plans may still be in flux and for those whose declared career goals allow for flexibility should their plans not work out. By introducing the idea of pencil planning, you will be able to re-enforce that goals are set at a point in time, based on the information available at that time, and within the context of the young person's circumstances—at that time. They may be reassured knowing that their pencil plans can be "erased" and re-written when new information surfaces or circumstances change.

Strategy: For young people who are fixated on a single career goal or are enrolled in an occupationally-focused program of studies, a more hands-on approach, in the form of contingency planning, may be in order. Many single-minded young adults don't have back-up plans because they've never seriously considered the possibility that their plans might not work out.

Having back-up plans as part of the overall planning process helps young people prepare psychologically for the possibility that, somewhere along the line, things won't pan out and there will need to be a change. The young person who screeches to a full stop because there is no Plan B spends more time and turmoil becoming re-energized and getting back on track. By contrast, the one who has formulated a Plan B can rebound more quickly and switch gears without losing too much momentum.

Working with young people who have a stated goal and action plan, you can introduce contingency planning by asking them to consider what might happen to change their plans. This is particularly important for any action steps that are not completely in their control. You can then ask them to identify what they would do if things don't go their way.

A classic example of this is the legions of young people who apply each year for the limited number of seats available in Canadian medical schools. For the hopeful physician-to-be, the question is what will they do if they aren't accepted? Ideally, this has been taken into consideration in the early stages of their planning so that they have a back-up plan if their application is rejected.

By engaging in contingency planning, the young person is prodded to think about what might be the unthinkable. It allows them to generate possible alternative routes, thus becoming a proactive anticipator instead of a passive victim of change.

Do What You Love Somewhere in Your Life

Popular press career guides and advice websites with words like "passion," "dream," and "love" in their titles help to keep the Career Myth fire stoked. They would have us believe that there are soul-lifting jobs for everyone; that everyone should strive to find theirs, and that there are "secrets" to be revealed that will ensure it happens. Sensational titles are good for sales. Not so good for offering realistic advice.

Young adults who fall victim to these messages often spend anxious years sifting through countless ideas and churning through countless jobs trying to "find" their passion. Unable to find fulfillment, they blame themselves for being unmotivated, responsible for the misery that has befallen them, or failing to live up to their potential.

Some people do love their jobs; others the polar opposite. Some have few expectations about their jobs beyond the pay, while others go through anguish in a never-ending pursuit of work that has meaning and purpose. Then there are those who love their work too much and let it consume their lives at the expense of everything else. The end results are commonly seen: burnout, ruined relationships, and regrets at some later point in time.

Most of us fall somewhere along the spectrum. We love or like the good parts of our jobs, suffer through the bad, and look for ways to find personal fulfillment in the hours we're not at work.

The quality of your life is improved immeasurably if you can find some avenue where you can do what you love—whether that's in your job or not. Since everyone has a different definition of living the dream, it can take some effort to figure out how to bring harmony to what can sometimes seem like two incompatibles: one's work and one's passions.

Strategy: A place to start is trying to debunk the notion that work should be the primary (or preferred) place where young adults find meaning in their lives. That expectation places a lot of pressure on young people to find jobs that are fulfilling and to be continually dissatisfied with the jobs they get.

Not everything that one is passionate about is marketable and, even if it is, the effort it takes to make and keep it marketable might take the passion out of it. As Jarrod commented, "I love gardening more than anything, but I would hate my life if I had to load up a truck everyday and garden people's lawns." In a case of "be careful what you wish for," young people need to seriously consider how strong their passion is and how much work they are prepared to put into turning a passion into a living.

If young adults can free themselves from expecting that their work should be their passion, they will be able to proceed on their career journeys with greater flexibility and less frustration. They can then give themselves rein to follow, however far, where their hearts lead them because they aren't under any pressure to make a living out of it. By doing something that they love long enough and good enough, it may come to pass that the money starts rolling in. But they shouldn't necessarily expect that to happen.

Strategy: Part of the "follow your passion" message suggests that passion is "out there," somewhere to be found. In reality, passion is an energy that we carry in us. If career professionals are able to help young people reposition their notion of passion to a simpler concept like "things that make me come alive," young people might find it easier to start looking within, rather than searching out there.

Those who are looking for passion in all the wrong places, those who worry that they don't have passion, and those who let passion play second fiddle to their work might be able to start imagining what some of those things actually are. They can start to think about what matters to them, what gets them excited, where their moments of greatest joy are, and what is so much a part of them that they have no choice but to do it. This gets to the nitty-gritty of what makes a person come alive.

By recognizing passions they already have or getting turned in the right direction, young people are more apt to begin noticing areas where their passions can be more fully expressed. Their need to find passion in their work may be lessened, or they may be able to start identifying areas in their work where passion can be introduced.

Strategy: For counselling professionals working with young people who seem to be driven solely by their jobs, the challenge is to help them bring some balance into their lives. This involves helping them identify other interests that have brought them great satisfaction in the past or current ones that are now getting short shrift. They also need to be helped to work out ways they can protect their personal time from the intrusions of work because that is something that's gotten away from them.

For those young people who find their work a necessary drudgery or for those who are vaguely discontented with the jobs they have, career professionals can guide them to see their jobs through a different lens. Where they are right now isn't forever and where they are right now can be improved.

Looking to charge one's passion can begin with transforming where they find themselves planted. What perks do they derive from their job? Have they looked hard and have they taken advantage of them? In what ways could they invest more of their true selves into their jobs? How could they inject more mastery or flair or incorporate a passion into the work they currently perform? How could they get involved in new aspects of the work within their organization that they really like? Have they tried?

They only need to look at making small changes because small changes can make a big difference. They go a long way to boosting a person's mood and helping them to de-stress and re-focus on the positive.

Strategy: Finding ways for young people to incorporate their passion into their lives requires crafting. Counselling professionals need to help young people craft an *overall* life design that allows them to live their passions, rather than putting all their energies into finding a career that will meet all their passions.

Barbara Sher offers a number of different crafting approaches that allow people to inject passion into their lives.[24]

- *Moonlighting:* Do what you love outside work hours. This strategy works best when it's something quite different from what you do as your day job, e.g. an information technologist who DJs on weekends.
- *Alternating goals:* Arrange your life so that you can devote a block of time to your pursuit, e.g. a month-long cycling trip or French immersion course.

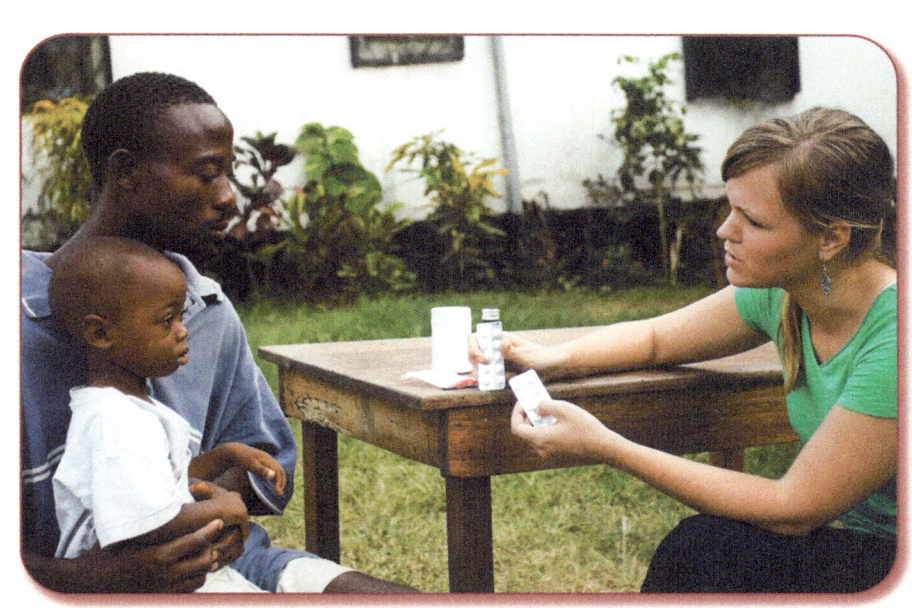

CHAPTER SIX 85

- *Multi-media goals:* Combine several goals into one, e.g. a nurse who is into social causes working for Doctors Without Borders or a counsellor who loves the outdoors leading wilderness trips with high-risk youth.
- *Main meals and side dishes:* Do something every once in awhile for pleasure, e.g. weekly ceramics class, get-away ski weekends, or entering chess tournaments.

Parting Words

In closing, this book has demonstrated that we as career professionals and young people themselves need to acknowledge that uncertainty and change are inherent parts of most young adults' career journeys. Many of us wish it were otherwise. Margaret Wheatley, a well-respected writer and organizational development consultant, speaks to the difficulties of dealing with the contingencies of career pathways, not only for young people, but for all of us.

This need to discover for ourselves is unnerving. I keep hoping I'm wrong and that someone, somewhere, really does have the answer. But I know we don't inhabit that universe any longer. In this new world, you and I have to make it up as we go along, not because we lack expertise or planning skills, but because that is the nature of reality. Reality changes shapes and meaning as we're in it. It is constantly new. We are required to be there, as active participants. It can't happen without us, and nobody can do it for us.[25]

It is imperative for career professionals to take into account the fact that many young people's career pathways are subject to unpredictability and change. Of all the things that young people need to assist them in the decade after high school, perhaps the most important is the support and patience of family members and professionals while they engage in the process of crafting a career in a complex and unpredictable environment.

Notes

Chapter One

1. Andy Furlong, "Introduction: Youth in a Changing World," *International Social Science Journal* 52 (2000): 129-134.

   Jane Higgins and Karen Nairn, "'In Transition': Choice and the Children of New Zealand's Economic Reforms," *British Journal of Sociology of Education* 27:2 (2006): 207-220.

2. See, for example, Randall Collins, "The Dirty Little Secret of Credential Inflation," *The Chronicle of Higher Education* (September 2002). http://chronicle.com/weekly/v49/i05/05b02001.htm (accessed May 3, 2007).

3. See, for example, Maritime Provinces Higher Education Commission, (MPHEC), *Five Years On: A Survey of the Class of 2003* (Fredericton, NB: MPHEC, 2010). http://www.mphec.ca/resources/FiveYearsOn_GFU_2008En.pdf (accessed September 18, 2014).

4. Jeffrey Jensen Arnett, "Emerging Adulthood: A Theory of Development from the Late Teens Through the Twenties," *American Psychologist* 55 (2000): 469–480.

   Jeffrey Jensen Arnett, *Emerging Adulthood: The Winding Road from the Late Teens Through the Twenties* (New York: Oxford University Press, 2004).

5. "Milling and churning" is a term that the OECD has used to describe a process in which young people move between or combine various activities such as full-time work, part-time work, study, unemployment, or other activities such as travelling. Organisation for Economic Co-operation and Development. *From Initial Education to Working Life: Making Transitions Work* (Paris: Author, 2000).

6. Canadian Federation of Students (CFS), *Student Debt in Canada: Education Shouldn't be a Debt Sentence* (Ottawa: CFS, 2013). http://cfs-fcee.ca/wp-content/uploads/sites/2/2013/11/Factsheet-2013-11-Student-Debt-EN.pdf (accessed August 14, 2014).

7. Ibid.

8. Danielle Shaienks and Tomasz Gluszynski, *Participation in Postsecondary Education: Graduates, Continuers and Drop Outs, Results from YITS Cycle 4* (Ottawa: Minister of Industry, 2007).

9. Organisation for Economic Co-operation and Development, *Canada Country Note—Education at a Glance 2012: OECD Indicators*, http://www.oecd.org/canada/EAG2012%20-%20Country%20note%20-%20Canada.pdf (accessed June 24, 2014).

10. Shaienks and Gluszynski, *Participation in Postsecondary Education*.

11. Ibid.

12. MPHEC, *Five Years On*.

13. Canadian Council of Learning (CCL), *Tallying the Costs of Post-secondary Education: The Challenge of Managing Student Debt and Loan Repayment in Canada* (Ottawa: CCL, 2010). http://www.ccl-cca.ca/CCL/Reports/PostSecondaryEducation/PSEHome/PSEChallengesMonograph3.html (accessed June 15, 2014).

14. CFS, *Student Debt in Canada*.

15. This amount was calculated on Canlearn's Loan Payment Estimator. It was premised on a 3% fixed rate of interest. http://tools.canlearn.ca/cslgs-scpse/cln-cln/crp-lrc/calculer-calculateeng.do;jsessionid=a032fbf67813f25f689ad68170651597dd0979f704f5c152b24a519f521b3342.e34Rc3iMbx8Oai0Tbx0SaxqPchj0 (accessed August 28, 2014).

16. Sharanjit Uppal and Sébastien LaRochelle-Côté, *Overqualification Among Recent University Graduates in Canada* (Statistics Canada, April, 2014). http://www.statcan.gc.ca/pub/75-006-x/2014001/article/11916-eng.htm (accessed July 14, 2014).

17. Peter Dwyer, Graeme Smith, Debra Tyler, and Johanna Wyn, *Immigrants in Time: Life-Patterns 2004* (Melbourne, Australia: Australian Youth Research Centre, 2005). web.education.unimelb.edu.au/yrc/linked_documents/RR27.pdf (accessed October 15, 2009).

18. Karen Vaughan, "The Pathways Framework Meets Consumer Culture: Young People, Careers, and Commitment," *Journal of Youth Studies* 8:2 (2005): 173-186, p.181.

19. Georgia T. Chaio and Philip D. Gardner, "Today's Young Adults: Surfing for the Right Job" (prepared for MonsterTRAK, 2007). http://ceri.msu.edu/ publications/pdf/YAdults-16.pdf (accessed May 15, 2009).

20. Dwyer et al., *Immigrants in Time*.

21. Arnett, "Emerging Adulthood: A Theory of Development."

    Arnett, *Emerging Adulthood: The Winding Road*.

22. Dwyer et al., *Immigrants in Time*.

23. Arnett, *Emerging Adulthood: The Winding Road*.

    Ingrid Schoon, Andy Ross, and Peter Martin, "Sequences, Patterns, and Variations in the Assumption of Work and Family-related Roles: Evidence from Two British Birth Cohorts" in *Transitions from School to Work: Globalization, Individualization, and Patterns of Diversity*, eds. Ingrid Schoon and Rainer K. Silbereisen, 219-242 (Cambridge, UK: Cambridge University Press, 2009).

24. Arnett, "Emerging Adulthood: A Theory of Development."

    Arnett, *Emerging Adulthood: The Winding Road*.

25. Employment and Social Development Canada, *Indicators of Wellbeing in Canada—Family Life-Marriage*. http://www4.hrsdc.gc.ca/.3ndic.1t.4r@-eng.jsp?iid=78_(accessed June 24, 2014).

26. Arnett, "Emerging Adulthood: A Theory of Development."

27. Ibid.

    Dwyer et al., *Immigrants in Time*.

    Karen Vaughan and Josie Roberts, "Developing a 'Productive' Account of Young People's Transition Perspectives, *Journal of Education and Work* 20:2 (2005): 91-105.

28. Hanoch Flum, and David L. Blustein, "Reinvigorating the Study of Vocational Exploration: A Framework for Research, " *Journal of Vocational Behavior* 56:3 (2000): 380-404.

    Seth J. Schwartz, James E. Côté,, and Jeffrey J. Arnett, "Identity and Agency in Emerging Adulthood: Two Developmental Routes in the Individualization Process," Youth & Society 37:2 (2005): 201-229.

29. Dwyer et al., *Immigrants in Time*.

    Bill Law, Frans Meijers, and Gerard Wijers, "New Perspectives on Career and Identity in the Contemporary World," *British Journal of Guidance & Counselling* 30:4 (2002), 431-449.

30. Flum and Blustein, "Reinvigorating the Study of Vocational Exploration."

    Jeffrey Jensen Arnett, "The Concept of Emerging Adulthood," in *Readings on Adolescence and Emerging Adulthood*, ed. Jeffrey Jensen Arnett, 17-31 (Upper Saddle River, New Jersey: Prentice Hall, 2002).

    David L. Blustein, "A Context-rich Perspective of Career Exploration Across the Life Roles," *Career Development Quarterly* 45:3 (1997): 260-274.

31. Flum and Blusten, "Reinvigorating the Study of Vocational Exploration," 393.

32. Jennifer Bryce and Michelle Anderson, "What Can Be Learned from The Roller Coaster Journeys of Young People Making Ultimately Successful Transitions Beyond School?," *Australian Journal of Career Development* 17:1 (2008): 41-49.

    Steven J. Ball, Shelia Macrae, and Meg Maguire, "Young Lives, Diverse Choices and Imagined Futures in an Education and Training Market," *International Journal of Inclusive Education* 3:3 (1999): 195-224.

    Barbara Schneider and David Stevenson, *The Ambitious Generation: America's Teenagers, Motivated but Directionless* (New Haven, CT: Yale University Press, 1999).

33. Ball et al., "Young Lives, Diverse Choices, and Imagined Futures," 209.

34. Ibid.

35. Phil Hodkinson, Andrew C. Sparkes, and Heather Hodkinson, *Triumphs and Tears: Young People, Markets and the Transition From School To Work* (London: David Fulton Press, 1996).

36. Thomas S. Krieshok, "How The Decision-Making Literature Might Inform Career Center Practice," *Journal of Career Development* 27:3 (2001): 207-216.

37. Karen Evans, "Concepts of Bounded Agency in Education, Work, and the Personal Lives of Young Adults," *International Journal of Psychology* 42:2 (2007): 85-93.

38. Vaughan and Roberts, "Developing a 'Productive' Account."

39. David L Blustein, "Extending the Reach of Vocational Psychology: Toward an Inclusive and Integrative Psychology of Working," *Journal of Vocational Behavior* 59:2 (2001): 171-182.

    Mary Sue Richardson, "Work in People's Lives: A Location for Counseling Psychologists," *Journal of Counseling Psychology* 40 (1993): 425-433.

40. Tom Zizys, *An Economy Out of Shape: Changing the Hourglass* (Toronto: The Toronto Workforce InnovationGroup, 2012), http://www.theconstellation.ca/img_upload/08acc0993e95b9dd86af3df3ef8e7c51/EconomyOOShape.pdf (accessed July, 12 2014).

41. Sharanjit Uppal and Sébastien LaRochelle-Côté, *Overqualification Among Recent University Graduates in Canada* (Statistics Canada, April, 2014). http://www.statcan.gc.ca/pub/75-006-x/2014001/article/11916-eng.htm (accessed July 14, 2014).

42. See for example, MPHEC, *Five Years On*.

43. See for example, Canadian Education and Research Institute of Canada (CERIC), *Career Development in the Canadian Workplace: National Business Survey*. http://ceric.ca/?q=en/node/805 (accessed September 18, 2014).

44. Rick Miner, "The Great Canadian Skills Mismatch: People Without Jobs, Jobs Without People and MORE (Miner Management Consultants, 2014). http://www.minerandminer.ca/data/Miner_March_2014_final(2).pdf (accessed 14 July, 2014).

45. Alan C. Kerckhoff, "The Transition from School to Work," in *The Changing Adolescent Experience Boston*, eds. Jeylan T. Mortimer & Reed W. Larson , 52-85 (New York: Cambridge University Press, 2002).

46. Peter Cappelli, *Why Good People Can't Get Jobs: The Skills Gap and What Companies Can Do About It* (Philadelphia: Wharton Digital Press, 2012).

47. Sophie Borwein, *Bridging the Divide, Part I: What Canadian Job Ads Said* (Ottawa: Higher Education Quality Council of Ontario, 2014). http://www.heqco.ca/SiteCollectionDocuments/Skills%20Part%202.pdf (accessed December 7, 2014).

48. Roderic Beaujot and Don Kerr, *Emerging Youth Transition Patterns in Canada: Opportunities and Risks* (Ottawa: Policy Research Initiative, Government of Canada, 2007). http://ir.lib.uwo.ca/pscpapers/vol21/iss5/1/ (accessed July 29, 2009).

    Warren Clark, "Delayed Transitions of Young Adults," *Canadian Social Trends* 84 (September 18, 2007): 14-22. http://www.statcan.gc.ca/daily-quotidien/070918/dq070918b-eng.htm (accessed September 15, 2014).

49. Poverty and Employment Precarity in Southern Ontario (PEPSO) Research Group, *It's More Than Poverty: Employment Precarity and Household Well-being in Southern Ontario* (Toronto: PEPSO, 2013). http://s3.documentcloud.org/documents/607642/its-more-than-poverty-summary-final-2013-02-09.pdf (accessed August, 14 2014).

50. Certified General Accountants Association of Canada, *Youth Employment in Canada: Challenging Conventional Thinking.* http://www.cga-canada.org/en-ca/ResearchReports/ca_rep_2012-10_youthunemployment.pdf (accessed September 1, 2014).

51. Arnett, "Emerging Adulthood: A Theory of Development."

52. Wendy Patton and Mary McMahon, *Career Development and Systems theory: A New Relationship* (Pacific Grove, CA: Brooks/Cole, 1999).

53. Deborah G. Betsworth, and Jo-Ida C. Hansen, "The Categorization of Serendipitous Career Development Events," *Journal of Career Assessment* 4 (1996): 91-98.

    Jim E.H. Bright, Robert G.L. Pryor and Lucy Harpham, "The Role of Chance Events in Career Decision Making," *Journal of Vocational Behavior* 66:3 (2005): 561-576.

54. John D. Krumboltz and Al S. Levin, *Luck is No Accident: Making the Most of Happenstance in Your Life and Career* (Atascardo, CA: Impact Press, 2004).

55. Stephen F. Hamilton, *Apprenticeship for Adulthood: Preparing Youth for the Future* (New York: Free Press, 1990).

    Neil Howe and William Strauss, *Millennial's Rising: The Next Great Generation* (New York: Vintage Books, 2000).

    Schneider and Stevenson, *The Ambitious Generation*.

    James E. Côté, *Arrested Adulthood: The Changing Nature of Maturity and Identity* (New York: New York University Press, 2000).

56. Cathy Campbell, "A Study of the Career Pathways of Canadian Young Adults During the Decade After Secondary School Graduation" (PhD diss., Massey University, New Zealand, 2011).

57. Jane Higgins, "Young People and Transitions Policies in New Zealand," *Social Policy Journal of New Zealand* 18 (2002): 44-61.

58. Phyllis Moen and Patricia Roehling, *The Career Mystique: Cracks in the American Dream* (Lanham, MA: Rowman & Littlefield, 2005).

    Phyllis Moen, "Careers," in *Encyclopedia of the Life Course and Human Development*, vol. 2, Adulthood, ed. Deborah S. Carr, 37-40 (Detroit: Macmillan Reference USA, 2009).

59. Heather Carpenter, *The Career Maze: Guiding Your Children Towards a Successful Future* (Auckland, New Zealand: New Holland, 2008).

60. Campbell, "A Study of the Career Pathways of Canadian Young Adults."

61. Ibid.

62. Teresa E. McAlpine, "College Students and Career: An Exploration of Vocational Anticipatory Socialization" (PhD diss., University of North Carolina at Chapel Hill, 2009). https://cdr.lib.unc.edu/indexablecontent/uuid:fc87c8d0-daae-40a6-84a5-9de95b331e8e http://media.proquest.com/media/pq/classic/doc/1574154221/fmt/ai/rep/NPDF?_s=XSp1YN%2FVas6zgP9%2FfAPmpDEw9QU%3D (accessed December 15, 2010).

63. Robert G.L. Pryor and Jim E. Bright, "Applying Chaos Theory to Careers: Attraction and Attractors." *Journal of Vocational Behavior* 71:3 (2007): 375-400.

64. Jim E. Bright and Robert G.L. Pryor, "Shiftwork: A Chaos Theory of Careers Agenda for Change in Career Counseling." *Australian Journal of Career Development* 17:3 (2008): 63-72. p. 68.

65. Moen, "Careers."

66. John D. Krumboltz, "The Wisdom of Indecision," *Journal of Vocational Behavior*, 41(1992): 239-244.

67. Krieshok, "How The Decision-making Literature Might Inform Career Center Practice," 213.

68. Jenn Davies, "Notes from the Ethics of Career 'Planning,'" *CCPA Career Counsellors' Chapter Blog,* entry posted February 1, 2014, http://ccpacdchapter.blogspot.ca/2014/02/notes-from-ethics-of-career-planning.html (accessed September 14, 2014).

69. J.N. Salter, "My 20s Weren't Supposed to Be Like This: Getting Through the Quarter-Life Crisis," *The Blog*, entry posted February 4, 2014, http://www.huffingtonpost.com/jn-salters/quarterlife-crisis-is-tha_b_5072177.html (accessed August 15, 2015).

Chapter Two

1. The word "strategy" implies a level of intentionality and proactivity that was not typical of the behavior of the young people who participated in this study. As will be explained in later chapters, strategies generally emerged from a convergence of factors rather than being chosen. However, we have chosen to use the word "strategies" here because there did not seem to be a word that more comprehensively encapsulated their actions.

2. Amy Wrzesniak, Clark McCauley, Paul Rozin, and Barry Schwartz, "Jobs, Careers, and Callings: People's Relations to Their Work," *Journal of Research in Personality* 31:1 (1997): 21-33.

Chapter Three

1. Peter L. Benson, "Developmental Assets and Asset-building Community: Conceptual and Empirical Foundations," in *Developmental Assets and Asset –Building Communities: Implications for Research, Policy, and Practice*, eds. Richard M. Lerner and Peter L. Benson, 19-46 (New York: Kluwer Academic/Plenum Publishers, 2003).

Chapter Six

1. Campbell, "A Study of the Career Pathways of Canadian Young Adults."

2. Mark J. Miller, "A Case for Uncertainty in Career Counseling." *Counseling and Values* 39:3 (1995): 162-168.

3. H. B. Gelatt, "Positive Uncertainty: A New Decision-Making Framework for Counselling," *Journal of Counselling Psychology* 36:2 (1989): 252-256.

    H. B. Gelatt, "Future Sensing: Creating the Future," *The Futurist* 27:5 (1993): 9-13.

H. B. Gelatt, "Chaos and Compassion." *Counseling and Values* 39 (1995): 108-116.

H. B. Gelatt and Carol Gelatt, *Creative Decision Making: Using Positive Uncertainty* (Boston: Thomson Crisp Learning, 2003).

4. John D. Krumboltz, Anita Mitchell, and Brian Jones, "A Social Learning Theory of Career Selection," *The Counselling Psychologist* 6:1 (1976): 71-80.

   John D. Krumboltz and Charles W. Nichols, "Integrating the Social Learning Theory of Career Decision Making," in *Career Counseling: Contemporary Topics in Vocational Psychology*, eds. W. Bruce Walsh and Samuel H. Osipow, 159-192 (Hillsdale, NJ: Lawrence Erlbaum Associates Inc., 1990).

   Linda K. Mitchell and John D. Krumboltz, "Krumboltz's Learning Theory of Career Choice and Counseling," in *Career Choice and Development*, 4th ed., eds. Duane Brown and Linda Brooks, 233-280 (San Francisco: Jossey-Bass, 1996).

5. Kathleen E. Mitchell, Al S. Levin, and John D. Krumboltz, "Planned Happenstance: Constructing Unexpected Career Opportunities," *Journal of Counseling and Development* 77 (1999): 115-124.

   John D. Krumboltz and Al S. Levin, *Luck is No Accident: Making the Most of Happenstance in Your Life and Career* (Atascardo, CA: Impact Press, 2004).

6. Danielle Riverin-Simard, *Work and Personality* (Montreal: Meridien, 1998).

   Danielle Riverin-Simard, *Key Roles in the Revolution of Work* (Ottawa: Canadian Career Development Foundation, 1999).

   Danielle Riverin-Simard, "Career Development in a Changing Context of the Second Part of Working Life," in *The Future of Career*, eds. Audrey Collin and Richard A. Young, 115-129 (Cambridge: Cambridge University Press, 2000).

7. Jim E. H. Bright and Richard G. L. Pryor, "The Chaos Theory of Careers: A User's Guide," *The Career Development Quarterly* 53:4 (2005): 291-305.

   Bright and Pryor, "Shiftwork."

   Robert G. L. Pryor, Norman E. Amundson, and Jim E. H. Bright, "Probabilities and Possibilities: The Strategic Counseling Implications of the Chaos Theory of Careers," *Career Development Quarterly* 56:4 (2008): 309-318.

   Robert G. L. Pryor and Jim E. H. Bright, "The Chaos Theory of Careers," *Australian Journal of Career Development* 12:2 (2003): 12-20.

   Robert G. L. Pryor and Jim E. H. Bright, "Order and Chaos. A Twenty-first Century Formulation of Careers," *Australian Journal of Psychology* 55:2 (2003): 121-128.

   Robert G. L. Pryor and Jim E. H. Bright, "Chaos in Practice: Techniques for Career Counsellors," *Australian Journal of Career Development* 14:1 (2005): 18-28.

   Robert G. L. Pryor and Jim E. H. Bright, "Counseling Chaos: Techniques for Practitioners," *Journal of Employment Counseling* 43:1 (2006): 2-17.

   Robert G. L. Pryor and Jim E. H. Bright, "Applying Chaos Theory to Careers: Attraction and Attractors," *Journal of Vocational Behavior* 71:3 (2007): 375-400.

8. Pryor, Amundson, and Bright, "Probabilities and Possibilities."

9. Katharine Brooks, *You Majored in What? Mapping Your Path from Chaos to Career* (New York: Penguin Group, 2009).

10. Hermina Ibarra, *Working Identity: Unconventional Strategies for Reinventing Your Career* (Boston: Harvard Business School Press, 2003).

11. Gray Poehnell and Norm Amundson, "CareerCraft: Engaging With, Energizing and Empowering Career Creativity," in *Career Creativity: Explorations in the Remaking of Work*, eds. Maury Peiperl, Michael B. Arthur, and N. Anand, 105-122 (Oxford University Press, 2002).

12. Mark L. Savickas, 2005. "The Theory and Practice of Career Construction" in *Career Development and Counseling: Putting Theory and Research to Work*, eds. Steven D. Brown and Robert W. Lent, 42-70 (Hoboken, NJ: John Wiley & Sons, 2005).

    Cathy Campbell and Michael Ungar, "Constructing A Life That Works: Part 1, Blending Postmodern Family Therapy And Career Counseling," *Career Development Quarterly* 53:1 (2004): 16-27.

    Cathy Campbell and Michael Ungar, "Constructing A Life That Works: Part 2, Blending Postmodern Family Therapy And Career Counseling," *Career Development Quarterly* 53:1 (2004): 28-40.

13. Campbell, "A Study of the Career Pathways of Canadian Young Adults."

14. Therese Schwenkler, "3 Things No One Tells You About Finding Your Life's Work," *Unlost Blog*, entry posted September 18, 2011, http://www.theunlost.com/work/3-things-no-one-tells-you-about-finding-your-lifes-work (accessed July 31, 2014).

15. The term "Shopping List" has been borrowed from the career development specialists at the Nova Scotia Community College who use the tool with clients as a way to delineate the elements that constitute satisfying work.

16. The term "Explore List" has been borrowed from the career development specialists at the Nova Scotia Community College who use the tool with clients as a way to generate a list of jobs, occupations, or work roles that are congruent with the most important elements identified on their "Shopping List."

17. Having a set of criteria, particularly one that relates to vocational personality, lessens the chances that young people will become overwhelmed by the choices that are available to them. Barry Schwartz contrasts the behaviour of "choosers," who had reference points for decision making, with "pickers," who selected from whatever was readily available, often without considering whether or not their choices were a good fit. Barry Schwartz, *The Paradox of Choice: Why Less is More* (New York: Harper Collins, 2004).

18. Norman E. Amundson, *Active Engagement*, 2nd ed. (Richmond, BC: Ergon Communications: 2003).

19. Mark Franklin, "CareerCycles: A Holistic and Narrative Method of Practice," in *Career Development Practice in Canada: Perspectives, Principles, and Professionalism*, eds. Blythe C. Shepard and Priya S. Mani, 441-464 (Toronto: Canadian Education and Research Institute of Counselling, 2014).

    Mark Franklin, "A Narrative Career Management Program that Increases Hope, Optimism, Confidence, Resilience: Outcome Study," *Career Convergence Magazine* (May 1, 2013) http://ncda.org/aws/NCDA/pt/sd/news_article/73013/_PARENT/layout_details_cc/false (accessed August 15, 2014).

20. Richard Wiseman, *The Luck Factor: Change Your Luck and Change Your Life* (New York: Hyperion, 2003).

21. Edward N. Drodge, "Career Counseling at the Confluence of Complexity Science and New Career," *M@n@gement* 5:1 (2002): 49-62.

    Pryor and Bright, "Applying Chaos Theory to Careers."

    Anna Miller-Tiedeman, "Personal Observations on Life Directions," *Journal of Counseling and Development* 66 (1988): 487-488.

22. Gelatt, "Chaos and Compassion."

23. Gelatt, "Future Sensing: Creating the Future."

24. Barbara Sher, *Wishcraft: How To Get What You Really Want* (New York: Ballantine, 1979).

25. Margaret J. Wheatley, *Leadership and the New Science: Discovering Order in a Chaotic World* (San Francisco: Berrett-Koehler, 1999).

Resources

Career Crafting Techniques

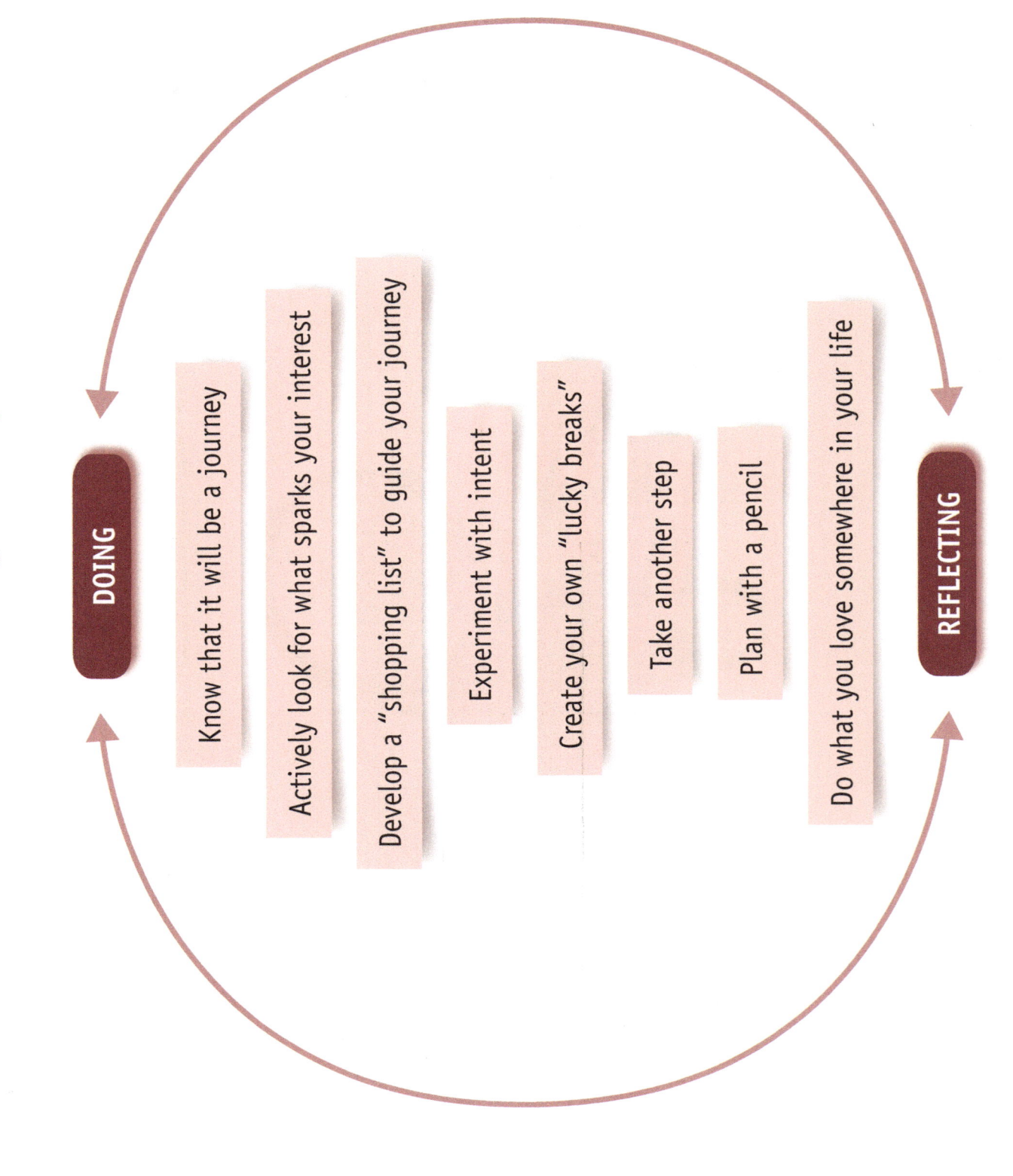

DOING → **REFLECTING**

- Know that it will be a journey
- Actively look for what sparks your interest
- Develop a "shopping list" to guide your journey
- Experiment with intent
- Create your own "lucky breaks"
- Take another step
- Plan with a pencil
- Do what you love somewhere in your life

The Career Myth

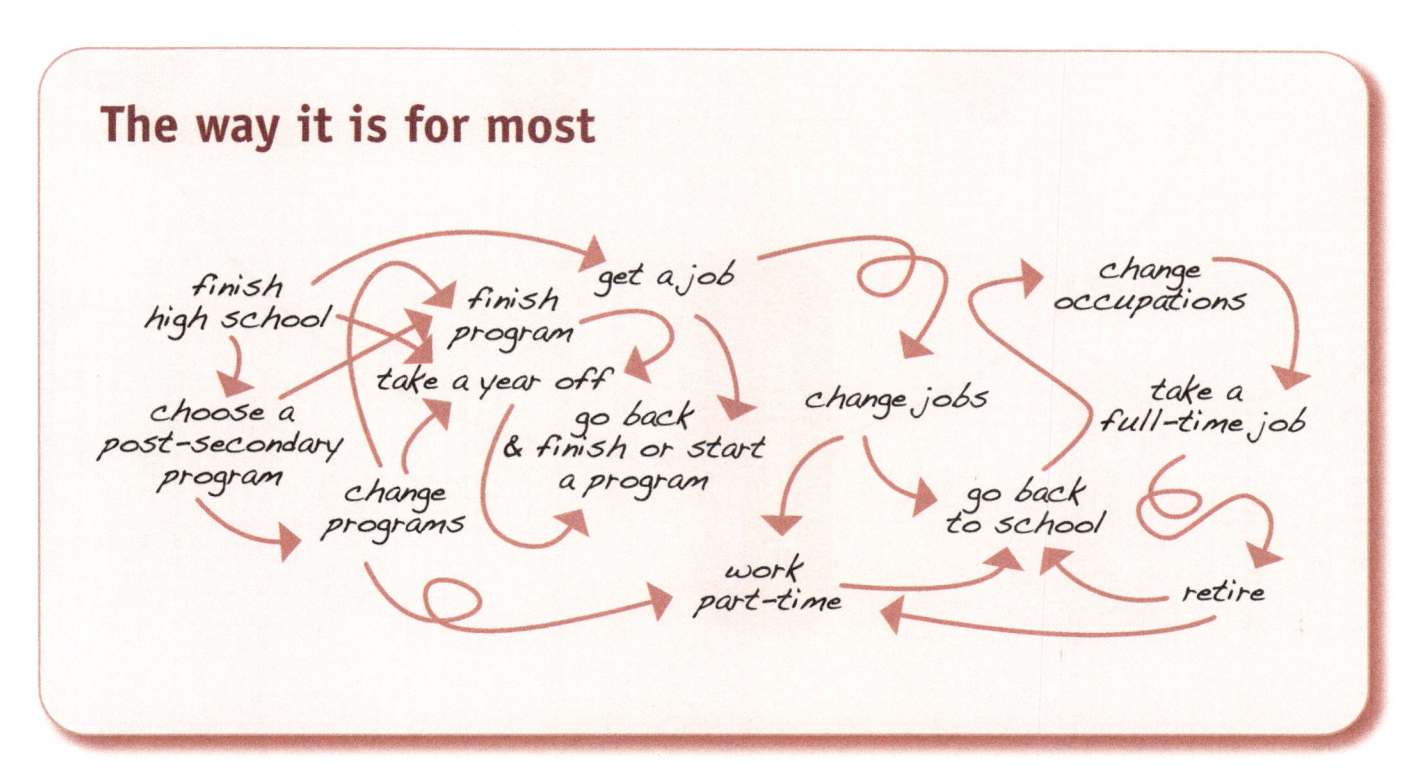

The way it is *supposed* to be

1. finish high school → 2. choose a post-secondary program → 3. finish the program → 4. get a job → 5. work → 6. retire

The way it is for most

finish high school, choose a post-secondary program, change programs, finish program, take a year off, go back & finish or start a program, get a job, change jobs, work part-time, go back to school, change occupations, take a full-time job, retire

This material is available courtesy of the Government of Alberta, Ministry of Innovation and Advanced Education.

RESOURCES 95

Finding Satisfying Work: Which Strategies Are You Using?

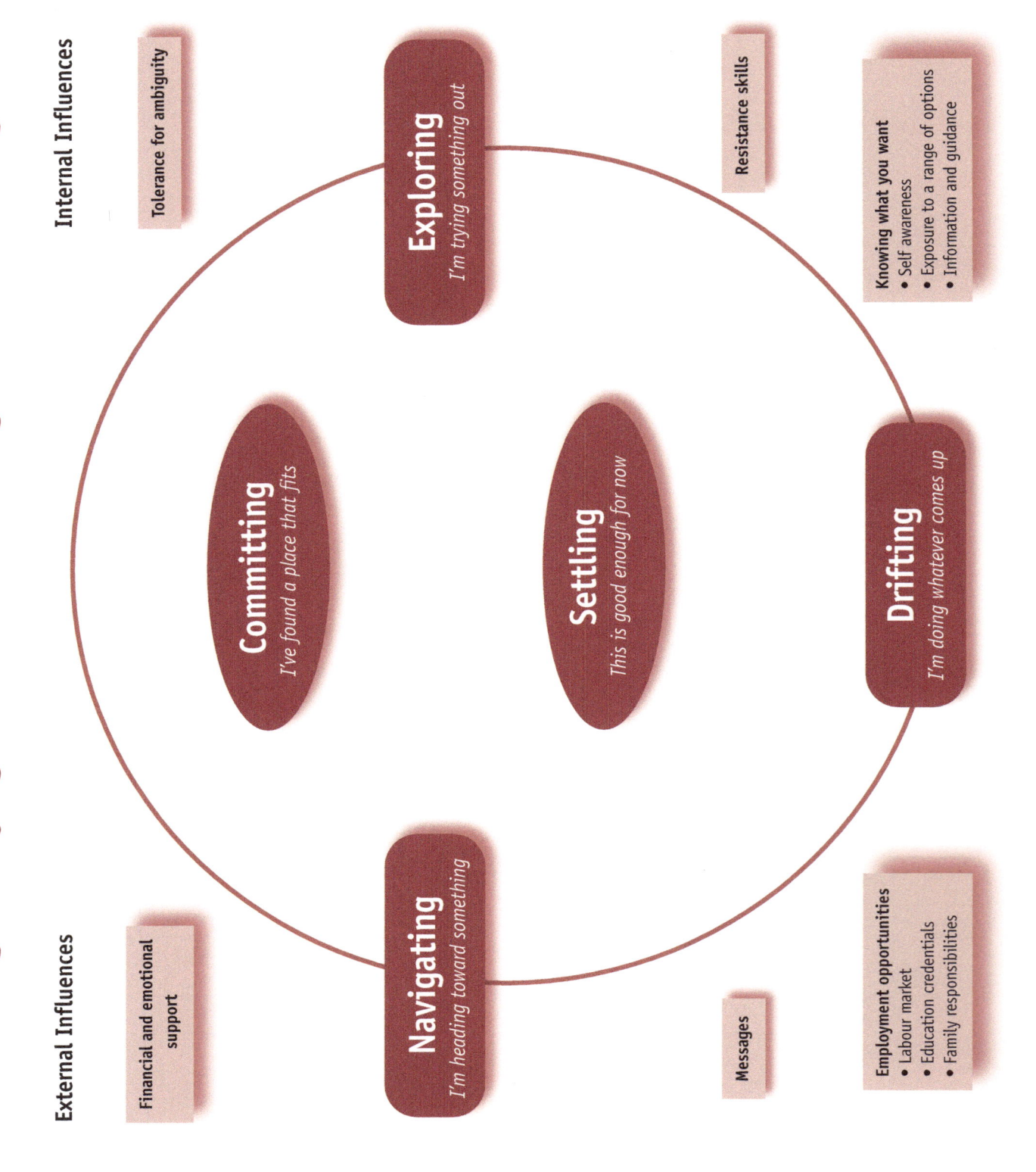

Internal Influences

- Tolerance for ambiguity
- Resistance skills
- **Knowing what you want**
  - Self awareness
  - Exposure to a range of options
  - Information and guidance

Exploring
I'm trying something out

Committing
I've found a place that fits

Settling
This is good enough for now

Drifting
I'm doing whatever comes up

Navigating
I'm heading toward something

External Influences

- Financial and emotional support
- Messages
- **Employment opportunities**
  - Labour market
  - Education credentials
  - Family responsibilities

Knowledge Champions

A very special thank you to the Knowledge Champions for career development who helped to support the publication of this educational resource.

Career Cruising

At Career Cruising (careercruising.com), we're on a mission to engage and inspire people of all ages and at all stages to achieve their full potential in school, career and life. We do this with an innovative self-exploration and planning program that engages people in the process of building their future. Visit our website and learn why more than 75% of schools and public libraries in Canada use Career Cruising with their students, teachers, parents and patrons.

Career Cycles

CareerCycles, professional career counselling, job search, resume/interview help for early-, mid-, late-career professionals. Gain confidence by accessing CareerCycles evidence-based narrative method, online tools and team of caring career professionals. Equally effective by phone, Skype, in-person in Toronto, Vancouver. Also: Training for helping professionals in our narrative method, and employee engagement programs for organizations.

GET STARTED with a free 15-minute career conversation! 1-844-465-9222 www.careercycles.com

Centre of Excellence in Financial Services Education

Toronto's financial services sector is projecting a need for people with the right skills and competencies in insurance, risk management, compliance, technology and business analysis, among others.

The Centre of Excellence in Financial Services Education works to strengthen Toronto's talent pool by conducting research on the sector's workforce needs; working with educators to align programs; and showcasing career opportunities. www.explorefinancialservices.com

CERIC

CERIC—the Canadian Education and Research Institute for Counselling—is a charitable organization that advances education and research in career counselling and career development. We support the creation of career counselling-related research and professional development for a cross-sectoral community through funding project partnerships and our strategic programs. These programs are Cannexus, ContactPoint/OrientAction, and *The Canadian Journal of Career Development*. www.ceric.ca

CES Career Education Society

The CES Career Education Society is a British Columbia based, non-profit organization of people in education, business, industry, labour, government and private organizations who work together to champion career and learning management as an essential life skill, with special emphasis on career education initiatives that benefit the province's youth. http://ces.bc.ca

Dalhousie University College of Continuing Education— University Preparation

Are you preparing for university?

Do you need to?

- Improve your marks?
- Earn a prerequisite to enter a specific university program?
- Build your confidence before taking a university credit course?

Please consult our website at www.dal.ca/faculty/cce/programs/university-preparation.html or email us at continuinged@dal.ca

Marine Institute of Memorial University

It's a big world. Be at the center of it. Welcome to the Marine Institute of Memorial University. We're a world-leading centre for marine and ocean-related career education and research. A cutting-edge education from the Marine Institute is one of the most affordable in Canada and gives you credentials that are recognized around the globe. www.mi.mun.ca

Memorial University of Newfoundland

Memorial University of Newfoundland has four campuses and over 19,000 students. The Memorial University experience goes beyond pure academics and invites a discovery of self, community and place. We celebrate our unique identity through the stories of our people—the work of our scholars and educators, the ingenuity of our students, the achievements of our alumni—and the impact we collectively make in our province, our country and our world. www.mun.ca

OSCA—Ontario School Counsellors' Association

The Ontario School Counsellors' Association leads the way in guidance and career education in Ontario. The new Education and Career/Life Planning Program has been designed to assist students in developing the knowledge and skills required to make informed career/life choices after secondary school. OSCA's What's Next Guide helps students find the information needed to make those choices. www.whatsnextguide.ca